PRAISE FOR

This Never Happened

"Liz Scott shares the achingly real struggle to understand her childhood and her narcissistic parents in her hilarious/beautiful/wrenching memoir, *This Never Happened*. Raging narcissism is the foundation of her confused childhood and continues into her acquiescent adulthood; there is no escape. She works hard to excavate the truth of her life, overturning each insane interaction with her parents; looking for answers, looking for meaning. Told with an unflinching willingness to self-examine, Scott never gives herself a pass on suspect behavior. It's no wonder Scott eventually becomes a therapist; her lifetime of ruthlessly analyzing her own life is a rich preparation for helping others. Told with raw humor, bracing humility, enough anger to light a fire, but ultimately with an abundance of love, *This Never Happened* is a deeply affecting and satisfying read. Brilliant!"

—**Dianah Hughley, Powell's Books**

"A remarkable hopscotch through memory and memorabilia to understand how the past shapes one's present. An irreverent, relatable, compulsively readable creation."

—**Robert Hill, author of *The Remnants***

"Spare, elegiac, *This Never Happened* is a mournful and yet reassuring memoir of a family's dissolution in the wake of a narcissistic mother and a father's abandonment. Liz Scott writes with warmth and humor, bringing light to even the saddest darkness. This memoir is destined to be a classic."

—Rene Denfeld, author of *The Child Finder*

"Surprising, funny, and impossible to put down, Liz Scott's memoir *This Never Happened* will break your heart with its calamitous wit and self-awareness. Scott's elusive pursuit of familial truth and belonging haunts every page. A strange, unforgettable search for meaning."

—Margaret Malone, author of *People Like You*

"In this unflinching memoir, Liz Scott gathers up the pieces of her family's legacy, from the exquisite yet heartbreaking letters young Liz wrote to the father who abandoned her, to the magnificent love letters between her parents before Liz was born—sentiments unrecognizable in the mutual rage Scott later witnessed for most of her life. Love and affection, when given at all, were doled out sparingly, and never without a price. *This Never Happened* is a searing examination of a life lived in the shadow of an unpredictable mother whose past remained hidden even on her deathbed, and whose motives for meanness seemed impossible to pin down. But Scott does just that, and in the process of cracking the code of her mother, it is Scott who breaks open and unfolds in this beautifully honest look at what it means to have compassion, however flawed, for the people who hurt us, and for whom we can never truly know or understand."

— **Deborah Reed, author of**
The Days When Birds Come Back

"Liz Scott's journey into the deep and vast is a journey into family. Who fits where and where is that place just for her. Where do I fit? Where do I belong? Liz takes a pickaxe to her illusions. Family. The deep and vast cavern where we smithy our chunk of coal into a diamond. You will love Liz Scott's memoir. Run out and buy it."

— **Tom Spanbauer, author of**
The Man Who Fell in Love with the Moon

THIS NEVER
HAPPENED

THIS NEVER HAPPENED

a memoir

LIZ SCOTT

HƎLL PꓤƎSS
UNIVERSITY OF HELL PRESS

This book is published by University of Hell Press
www.universityofhellpress.com

Interior Design by Olivia Croom
oliviacroomdesign.com

Cover Design by Gigi Little
gigilittle.jimdo.com

Published in the United States of America
ISBN 978-1-938753-31-2

For my parents, bless their hearts

"A woman has to be a daughter before she can be any kind of woman. If she doesn't have that in mind, if she doesn't know how to relate to her ancestors, to her tribe, she is not good for much."
—Toni Morrison

"Half the harm that is done in this world is due to people who want to feel important. They don't mean to do harm, but the harm (that they cause) does not interest them. Or they do not see it, or they justify it because they are absorbed in the endless struggle to think well of themselves."
—T.S. Eliot

"All happy families are alike: each unhappy family is unhappy in its own way."
—Leo Tolstoy

"Our parents are the ones who both wound us and administer the bandages."
—Anonymous

Contents

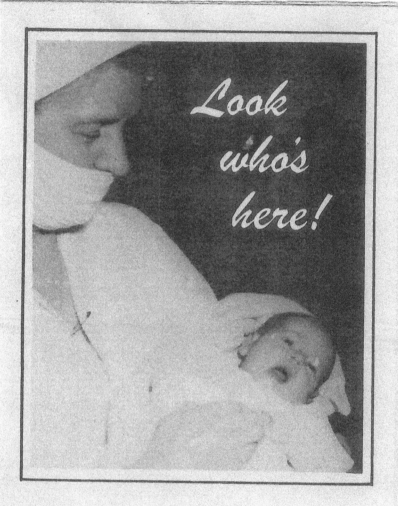

Look
who's
here!

1

To Begin

M Y MOTHER SAYS, "NOW'S THE TIME TO ASK. If you have any questions, now's the time." She waits till her deathbed to say this. It's hard to find the right adjective to describe how I feel, that it might be possible finally, after all this time, to get some answers to the mysteries of my family. Thrilling, shocking, flabbergasting, mind-bending, Jesus-fucking-christ, woman! It's been years—decades really—worrying this puzzle, this frustrating, vexing, bring-me-to-my-knees puzzle. What I know: I have a mother and a father. I have a sister. But that's hardly enough to construct even the outside border, let alone begin to fill in the picture.

* * *

Once when I was young I asked my mother if she had any brothers or sisters. Her answer: "I don't remember." That, in our family, passed for an acceptable, reasonable response. What the hell must be going on in a family where you just leave it at that? And then to boot, when my sister and I are already well into our adulthood—surprise! You're a Jew!

Now's the time to ask questions? Okay. Who am I? Where did I come from? How did you both—mother and father—get to be such fucking whack jobs, bless your hearts, but really.

I've come to believe that all of this—the facts about your ancestors, the truth about your family story, the reliable connections—are what create ballast in a life. With little to anchor me to earth, I've been in one long free float trying to forge some mooring in various ill-conceived ways with only modest success. Because really, before you clearly know what you're after, it's all mostly flailing. I'm into my eighth decade now and I imagine this is what happens when time starts to run out. The need to make sense becomes stronger and more urgent. If there are answers out there, I want them. If there is sense to be made, let me make it. And while we are at it, do let me forgive. Maybe. I guess. That's what I'm supposed to do, right?

*Leo and August Nelson are deliriously happy
to tell you of the birth of their daughter . . .*

ELIZABETH MIA NELSON

This paragon was born at the French Hospital on March 27, 1947, at 7:35 P.M. Her delivery, and her mother's care, were under the able guidance of Dr. Georgia Reid. She herself is now the charge of Dr. Sol N. Keen . . . There have been whispers in some quarters of other births and other babies. Her coming will, we hope, expose these rumors for the mischievous gossip they really are.*

THE PICTURE ON THE COVER

The shutter of the Speed Graphic snapped at the moment Elizabeth became four days old. She is behind the glass of the nursery, and in the arms of Mrs. Florence Powell—a woman well fitted for her job, if there ever was one.

*You understand of course that your own children, if any, are vigorously excepted.

Liz Scott   3

2

The Photograph (2005)

A LONG TIME AGO, PHOTOGRAPHS WERE SMALL and square. They were glossy black-and-whites with thin white borders and deckled edges. These days, if you even go the the trouble of printing a photo, it almost always has a date stamp. A long time ago it was left to the conscientious to take their fountain pen or quill to the back and date the event and, if they were thoughtful to posterity, tell me who the fuck that woman is.

The photo I found in my mother's file cabinet is a photo like that, small and square and aged with whitened creases. Not only is there nothing written on the back but even after taking a magnifying glass to it I can find nothing that gives me the slightest hint as to when, where, why, what, or who. It's a photograph of a woman. I can't tell how old she is because a long time ago pretty young looked pretty old so who knows. She faces the camera, staring straight out. Directly at me is where she's looking. She is dark haired and dark eyed. If it's possible for a face to have no expression, then she has none. I might not know who she is but I'm positive she is important to me. She is my grandmother. Or maybe my great-grandmother. Maybe this was taken the day before her family will immigrate to America and leave her behind. Or maybe it was her birthday and there was laughter and cake in the background because maybe this is what happy looked like in the shtetls. Maybe this was taken right before she was stolen away by the Cossacks. Or on her wedding anniversary. Or before the train took her away to die in the camps.

In the bathroom I hold the photograph next to my face to study the two of us in the mirror. Her hair is blackish like mine but no curls, though it's hard to tell, what with that severe style. We both have those dark, sunken eyes. A Semitic nose. I stare into her eyes and she just sits there, looking straight ahead, taunting me. She is mute and defiant. Speak, goddamn it! But she gives me nothing, just those staring eyes. Riveted on something beyond.

You, woman, are a reminder of what was stolen, not by the Cossacks or the S.S., but by my mother who knew exactly how to give and take all in one single gesture. It's not out of sentimentality that I keep this photograph. It's with vengeance and spite and masochism and the hope that if I hold on to her long enough, she will finally talk.

3

The Silver Ladle (1983)

Macy's in Union Square, San Francisco. My mother and I are shopping. This is what we do. We shop. We shop because here's the thing: you've got to drive there, look for parking, walk around, shop, stop for coffee, find the car, drive back. And all of that uses up a lot of time, time that otherwise might be *empty*, like time you'd need to fill by relating to each other or being gobsmacked by how very little relating you actually *want* to do. So we shop. We are in *Housewares*, having already been through *Cosmetics* and *Young Designers* and *Shoes* and *Accessories* and *Active Wear* and *Intimate Apparel* and *Big and Tall*. I'm looking at the china and the wine glasses and the serving dishes and then at my mother who is slipping a silver-ish ladle into her purse. "What the hell are you doing?" I say. "Put that back." Actually that's what I *feel* like saying but in there, right alongside my outrage, is the retroactive guilt about my own escapades as a teenage shoplifter—that and the fact that in our family we are very good at avoiding anything of substance. "Mother!" I say. My mother is free from shame. You have to hand it to her: she is completely devoid of that particular emotion, at least not in the way we humans think of it. When the shame was doled out in our family, she got none, my father got none, and my sister and I split the rest fifty/fifty. "I'm just going to *borrow* it," she says. "I'll return it." This is true. She will return it. But what she leaves out is that she'll return it *after* saying she got it as a gift and that, *sure*, it would be fine to get a store credit. So, add this to the long list of crap we don't deal with. We march out of the store, filched ladle in purse. My mother, the thief, and me, the coward and accessory to her crime.

4

—

Steep Hill (around 1957)

IT WAS IN THE HOUSE ON STEEP HILL ROAD so I must have been somewhere around nine or ten years old. We only lived in that house for a couple of strange years at most. It was a brief and unexplained move that made very little sense at the time. Now I know that my mother had to sell her beloved converted barn on Kettle Creek Road because my parents were getting divorced. Back than I was told a different story. Or no story at all, is more like it. All I remember is that my father was away. A lot. His absences were explained as extended business trips. He'd be gone weeks at a time, home for a day or two, sleeping on the sofa and then away again. Even so, you tell me *business trips*, I believe *business trips*. What I made of the sleeping on the sofa part, I can't tell you.

The only explanation about the move to the house on Steep Hill was just to try something different though even at the time it was clear that my mother was not exactly thrilled. No way could she hide her misery at leaving the house she loved, the postcard New England home with the ancient stone wall out front, the weeping willow that hung over the back patio, the two story slate-floor living room and the acres of deep woods out back. I had my own misery too, leaving Donna, my best friend, who lived across the street down the long, curvy driveway through her own deep woods. We had moved back and forth from her house to my house as one melded unit since we met waiting for the school bus on that first day of kindergarten. The new house was only a mile or so away but still.

The good thing about the house on Steep Hill was that is was just up the way from Felton's Pond. In the winter we kids would strap on our stiff white leather skates and fight each other over who got to be the end of the whip. We'd fly around the winter pond, boys and girls screaming and pushing and watching out for spots of thin ice.

But when I think of those couple of years in the Steep Hill house, Felton's Pond only comes to mind as an afterthought. Before I remember Felton's Pond, it's this: I am coming up the stairs about to turn the corner to go into my own bedroom and I hear voices from my mother's room on the right, her door open slightly. She's talking to two girls, sisters. I can't tell you why I think they were sisters. I just know they were. I can't tell you why I believe they were our cousins because no one said they were and there was no reason to believe we even *had* cousins. I just know they were. Nothing about them before or after this snippet of conversation remains for me, only a frozen moment, my mother and these two girls, standing in her bedroom, my mother in a half-whisper saying, "Don't tell Liz and Margaret."

In another family, hearing "Don't tell Liz and Margaret" could have been a secret about something fun and exciting: "We're having ice cream for dessert;" "We're going to the circus;" "I'm buying the girls a pony." But even then, even with just those five words, I knew it was not something fun and exciting but something dark and vaguely forbidding.

My sister and I didn't know we were Jews back then. Well, maybe we knew but we didn't *know*. That topic was never raised and we faithfully joined our friends at the Congregational Church on big Christian holidays. But there was this sense—I can't even explain it. It was more than the jars of pickled herring in the refrigerator, more than dinners of chicken livers and onions and the breakfasts of matzoh brei, though those are sure some clues for anyone paying the slightest bit of attention. Just this vague sense of ethnicity that not one of us was willing to talk about. So was that it, the big secret?

Whatever it was, no way did I want to know. Fingers in my ears. La-la-la, keep walking. I can't hear you. I do *not* want to know. I. Do. Not. Want. To. Know.

5

Visiting My Father, Part One (1978)

I‍T'S ONLY A NINETY-MINUTE FLIGHT TO JFK but between the time the seat belt light switches off and when it lights up again, I manage to fit in three Bloody Marys and four trips to the bathroom. It's a bumpy ride, inside and out. There's a book in my lap opened to the first page. *We are talking now of summer evenings in Knoxville, Tennessee.* But no book can distract me. I am wondering if he still wears a fedora, if he still smokes a pipe. I am wondering if his shirt will smell the same as it did when I used to sit in the dark of his closet, breathing in the day's white shirt. I am wondering exactly what it is I am feeling. *We are talking now of summer evenings in Knoxville, Tennessee.* "Excuse me, Miss. Another Bloody Mary, please."

* * *

In high school we used to drive to JFK just to sit around and watch the reunions. It was like being in the whole world at one time and one place. Chanel suits and saris, hijabs and hippies, black power and bell-bottoms. We made up stories about who was dreading the arrival or waiting for a stranger; how long since they'd seen each other and whether they would cry and kiss each other on the lips. Almost always there was drama: *I've missed you so much! You're finally here! Welcome home! Welcome to America! You look exactly the same! I didn't recognize you!*

Me, I'm looking for Gregory Peck. I have this photo of my father, posed, head cocked, looking pensive and smart, holding a pipe to his mouth with the smoke curling up in that beautiful gray of black and white photos, crisp white Madison Avenue shirt, black wavy hair, angular features. Who wouldn't be excited to be looking for Gregory Peck?

In one of her many professional forays, my sister worked as a private investigator. She and I lived so far apart, not exactly estranged but in that column, just less extreme. We knew very little of each other's wildly different lives but somehow I'd heard that she was working as a P.I. So, after my head stopped spinning and before it flew off completely, it was not such a shock to hear that she had been looking for our father, the man who'd gone AWOL about twenty years earlier without a peep from him since. She had been looking for him and she had found him! She had found him and she had gone to see him! Right then I hated her. I truly did. *He was mine. You had her and he was mine.* The way I comforted myself was to remember that sure, my sister was the one who found our father and she was the one to reunite with him first but that's only because she had so much anger and hurt and unresolved crap where he was concerned. He was an open, weeping wound in her life that she desperately needed to stitch up. That's the story I told myself. With me it was different. I had no wounds to heal. My father and I were connected in a kind of mystical bond that you people could never understand. So what that I hadn't seen or heard from him for two decades. He was mine.

So me and my Bloody Mary-addled legs and my flip-flopping stomach deplane, walk on the Jell-O ground of the jetway into the terminal, scanning the crowd for fedora, pipe, and a white Madison Avenue shirt. I'm too busy looking up to see the short, bald man approach and it's only after his arms are around my waist, his head nestled into my neck that I realize who this is.

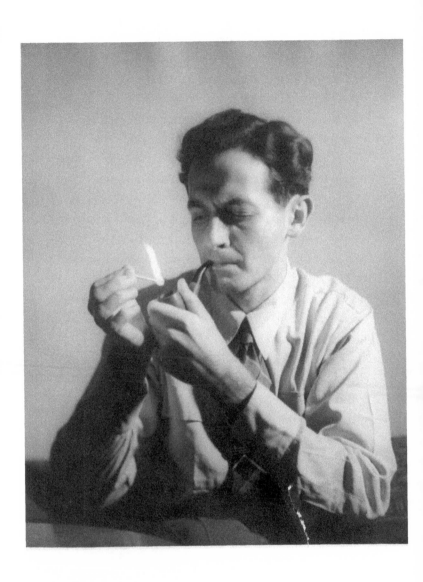

6

Ice Skating (around 1958)

You wait for the train on the platform at Saugatuck Station. Because it's cold, you wear your navy blue Chesterfield coat with the velvet collar. Because it's cold, you wear a white rabbit fur hat and matching muff for your hands. It's the first time you've taken the train by yourself and you repeat silently, *Slide the ticket under the metal tab on the seat behind your head; wait till the last stop to get off; go to the big clock in the terminal.*

You look for a seat by the window, choosing one where the maroon leather is not cracked and torn. No one sits next to you. It's just a little over an hour to the city but in your velvet drawstring purse is your new Christmas book, *Hidden Window Mystery*. Commuters read on the train—mostly newspapers, sometimes magazines—and you have saved this book for the trip.

The conductor lurches down the aisle and when he punches your ticket he sees that you are alone and stays a little longer at your seat. "Big date?" he says and you blush because this is what you imagine it feels like to be going on a date. "Ice skating," you say. "Rockefeller Center."

The spine of your book cracks when you open it, it's that new. *"Good-by, Hannah!" said Nancy Drew.* The train stops at Stamford, then Greenwich. Still your book is opened to the first page: *"Good-by, Hannah!" said Nancy Drew. She hugged the motherly, middle-aged housekeeper, then put a hand on the front door-knob.* Port Chester, Mamaroneck, Larchmont. Houses and stores and lampposts are green and red and silver and gold with Christmas. *She hugged the motherly, middle-aged housekeeper, then put a hand on the front door-knob. "Watch out for the falling tree branches," Hannah Gruen warned the attractive reddish-blond-haired girl.* Pelham. And finally Grand Central Terminal.

You follow the crowd up through the dark chill of the ramp into the massive terminal and it's easier to find the clock than you thought and easier to find him even with all the people. It's been awhile but you recognize the gray overcoat and gray felt hat with the black grosgrain ribbon. He smiles, throws his arm across your shoulder and says, "Let's take a taxi, princess."

Your table is at the edge of the ice so you can watch the skaters while you have your lunch. The tablecloth is stiff white linen and the menu has gold tassels and he says, "Whatever you want. Order anything," and he looks so hard into your eyes, like he's searching for something lost. Your cocoa and his martini come at the same time. *Fill the pitcher with ice and add a shot glass of gin; measure out a spoonful of dry vermouth and stir with the glass stick. Make sure no ice gets into the special thin-stemmed glass when you pour.* "I bet the ones I made you were better, right?" you say but now he's not looking at you at all and doesn't answer and you wonder if maybe you should ask again. Mothers and fathers and brothers and sisters circle the rink holding hands. Holiday happy. Silver and gold skaters with red-cheeked faces. Your cocoa is half gone and he hasn't had one sip of his drink yet, his eyes down, his face somehow falling, somehow getting darker. You say, "We're skating after lunch, right?" but still he doesn't answer. The air seems to get even more wintry and you wish you could put your coat back on but you are inside and in a restaurant and you can't remember the manners about that. He pulls the small paper napkin under his drink toward him and you can barely hear him when he says, "You need to understand." His head shakes from side to side and now his eyes are so low they are gone. "It's just too hard," he says, "…seeing you." There's a starched crease in the tablecloth and he runs his flat palms over and over it, working hard to smooth it out but no amount of smoothing makes it go away. The most important thing to him right now is to iron out that crease.

Out the window is a blur of faces, the flash of skate blades and the buildings, so many buildings. The city is right there and the buildings are so tall they sway in the ice gray winter sky, so tall you wonder what keeps them from falling.

7

What We Had

WE HAD SO MUCH.

We had woods that never stopped. We had creeks with tadpoles and garter snakes and painted turtles. We had real Indian arrowheads buried shallow in our backyards. We had freedom. We had mothers who didn't work. We had lessons: ballet and piano and horseback riding and ice-skating and ballroom dancing and etiquette. We had money. We had fathers who came home drunk on the 7:10 train or who stayed in the city during the week. We had swimming pools and tennis courts. We had no curfews. We had Zenobia and Mammy and Beulah and Miss Fay. We had rope swings over swimming holes.

We had real art on the walls and real antiques for furniture. We had mothers who took Miltown and stayed in bed all day. We had freezers packed with ice cream sandwiches and Eskimo Pies. We had no rules. We had spring vacations in the Caribbean. We had parents who had sex with our friends' parents. We had dogs and cats and horses and fish. We had camps we were sent to on the day after school let out that lasted until the day before it started again. We had famous neighbors. We had fathers who never came home. We had fireflies in mayonnaise jars with holes punched in the lids. We had ponies at birthday parties. We had friends' fathers who groped our small breasts. We had no chores. We had miles of twisty one-lane, stonewall-lined roads almost free of cars where we could ride our shiny bikes till dark. We had sex too early. We had cotillions. We had mountains of presents under the Christmas tree. We had perfect manners and perfect grammar. We had unlocked liquor cabinets and pantries stocked with cartons of Chesterfields. We had keys to the car before we had licenses and our own fancy cars to drive home from high school. We had dolls with full wardrobes, including real fur coats. We had illegal abortions in Park Avenue offices.

We had so much.

8

Dear Mother (around 1959)

THIS LETTER WAS THE ONE CHILDHOOD MEMENTO my mother kept, at least of mine. Maybe my sister has a big box of her toddler scribblings and letters from camp and lanyards and Mother's Day potholders. But this is it for me. I can see why my mother kept this letter. If one of my kids had ever written me such a thing I would surely preserve it and pull it out regularly to assuage myself and bask in the honorifics. I am grateful to have this letter. I am grateful for the evidence. I loved her. At one point I must have felt lucky that she was my mother. Not that it's the last time I felt love. Many times the feeling was there but only when I was not in her physical presence.

Bless her wounded heart, she always always *always* found a way to pull the rug right out from under any hint of softening.

Mother: how you made it so excruciatingly hard to love you.

Some people believe that we choose our parents. Literally choose them. That we have work to do on our own individual karmas in this life and that we pick exactly the people that will help us along on our journeys. Our parents—so goes the theory—are the ones who can best facilitate our emotional and spiritual growth, and not necessarily because they are ideal role models. Actually, quite the opposite. Whatever parental pathologies may exist are exactly what we need to move along on our path.

Well. Hmmm. I guess it would require that I believe in karma or past lives or Martians, which I am not quite sure I can do but I have to admit, there is some resonance. If someone asked me what my work was I would tell them that I see a girl who loves her mother and then I see the decades of anger and frustration and hurt and disappointment—so many years of shit piled so fuckingly high on top of that daughter-love. My life task: to clear away the shit and grant myself—us both really—the relief of compassion and forgiveness.

Dear Mother,

Its being Mother's day I am faced with the problem of choosing a worthy gift for you. This however is not difficult because I cannot buy anything (financial difficulties) and this eliminates one phase. *

I looked up the definition of mother in the dictionary and it has no specific qualifications pertaining to the behavior or quality of her children. This pleased me to no end; I was afraid you might not be a mother! But, fortunately, you are and quite a good one I might add. I can hear you now or at least hear what you are thinking----"But I have failed as a mother in bringing up you kids. It is my fault that you are selfish, egotistic, ..." and so forth , but go over the other types of mothers. We will take my friends' mothers as examples. First there is Mrs. M███. We'll need I say any more?! But her attitudes have effect on E███. Her prejudice and partial mind are poisoning E███. I am sure you have had enough experience with her to understand so I shall end with Mrs. M███. Next we will take Mrs. B██; very sweet, agreeable, abliging......thats it! She is much toooooo! D███ is as spoiled as a rotten apple or a piece of moldy bread. Now, Mrs. Z███. Protectiveness to a MASSIVE extent, that is her vice. She acts as if every step which S███ takes out of her house will be her last. Some things can go tooooo far........Mrs. E███ next. Quite lazy if you don't mind me saying..."D█, run in and get me some ice cubes;;;;go up and get me the bandaids, ███.....Change the station please....Turn of the stove, sugah..." and so on, EVERY MINUTE. I am just waiting for D██ to erupt, expecting the straw that broke the camel's back! Now let's see...ah yes, Mrs. B███ quite unaware as we once noticed. Also, consider the cause of her ulcer...! Mrs. B████, I think expects an angel to emmerge from a typical teenager, she is living quite a ways back if you know what I mean. Let us move on to Mrs. G████ (spelling?) . From what we both can see it is quite evident that Mrs. G. doesn't give a da...rn about her children. Quite frankly I think she is somewhat of a status seeker.

You have read here a brief summation of the OTHER types of mothers, that is the wrongkind. Don't be modest! Admit it, you are TOPS!!!! If you will permit me I shall list a ofsome of your past achievements.

Sewing
singing
dancing
acting
designing
photography
writing

Is that it? I doubt it. OH!?*! I forgot one......CHILDBIRTH... I believe this is your best field.

---

* This will have to do

9

Questions (2005)

IN THE AFTERNOON OF THE DAY BEFORE THE LAST day, when there was still some deluded possibility, my mother spoke her first words of the day. For the hours till then—the long hours through nurses coming in and out, with trays of obscenely useless food and pills that made no sense whatsoever—through phone calls with my kids, and my sister and I taking turns to the bathroom, and out to the hall to check email and voicemail—my mother just lay there stubbornly refusing to speak. Stubbornly refusing to die. I know how that must sound but trust me, it was a stubborn, selfish effort of will. Of course her stubbornness was no surprise but whatever else was lost for good, my mother retained her ability to amaze me. When my sister was out of the room for her mid-afternoon coffee break, my mother opened her eyes and said this: "If you have any questions, now's the time to ask." Just to put this in context, this from the woman who never gave up a shred of factual information about her past or her family—nothing, nada, niente, zip. You have no idea just how amazing this bold statement was.

I wonder now if my mother planned it that way, waiting till my sister was gone to make that tantalizing and completely out of character statement. My sister had always been closer to our mother. Always. She was willing to interact in ways that I never was—confiding in her, expressing her anger or hurt, fighting, hanging up, taking money, at least that's how it seemed to me. Growing up it was the two of them as a unit, me choosing to throw in my lot with a long-gone father. It had obviously seemed a better choice to me, teaming up with a gone person on whom I could project any old quality that suited my mood. I painted a picture of him with glitter and rainbows and unicorns and that pretty picture helped me resist what felt like the gravitational field that was my mother and sister. I have spoken with righteous pride about my near-toddler decision to separate myself from whatever wacky dance my mother and sister had going and choose the absent and invisible nut job instead. Still, when my mother said that—*If you have any questions, now's the time to ask*—I felt somehow anointed. My sister was out of the room and it was me. *Me.* How irresistible the need for parental approval. How enduring!

We are all opaque to each other to some infuriating degree. That I have unanswered questions doesn't make me special. *Did you hear that, self?* It does *not* make me special. In my defense though, it's like my small family of originally four—very soon after to be three—was plopped down on earth, manufactured in a lab somewhere, or dreamed up by some almighty who knows who. We came from no one and we were attached to no one. I could make that sound like a bad thing but I have worn my rootlessness like a custom-made, one-of-a-kind, jewel-encrusted cloak adorned with shiny medals that read "grandparent-less," "aunt-less," "uncle-less," "cousin-less." I say I have a gypsy soul. I like the sound of that, all wild and romantic. But a gypsy probably does not crave to fill in all the blank spaces. A gypsy probably does not feel the black absence of tap rootedness or the peril of floating off, untethered, into dark space. As it turns out, having questions is what defines me.

I scraped the metal chair across hospital linoleum up to the side of her bed. Boy oh boy, did I have questions.

10

Deep Cover

IN 1947, PRINCESS ELIZABETH MARRIED PRINCE Philip, her younger sister, Margaret, an attendant. Also in 1947 I, Elizabeth, was born and in 1953 came *my* sister, Margaret. Elizabeth and Margaret. Could that sound any more Anglican? In our school years we lived in a bucolic enclave in Connecticut, a commuter's train ride from New York City. We took horseback riding lessons, English saddle. Ballet with Miss O'Neil. Piano with Ruth Steinkraus, she of the New York Philharmonic. Ballroom dancing with Miss Bolyn, Russian, who wore a midnight blue cocktail sheath with black illusion at the bust and played "Fascination" on the stereo while we white-gloved boys and girls—those of whom had not gone off to boarding school—learned the fox trot. *Forward... forward... side together... back... back.* We started French and Latin in third grade and every home had both Emily Post and Amy Vanderbilt. We said "ahnt" and "tomahto." We learned where the fish knife went and the dessert spoon and that the knife blade always faces the plate. We played croquet and learned bridge. Every year my mother ran the antique fair at the Northfield Congregational Church, a postcard white clapboard and steepled church on a hill in a postcard of a New England town. And every year we attended church on Easter and Christmas, my sister and I wearing matching flowered dresses and matching bonnets on our curly heads in spring; Chesterfield coats and white rabbit fur muffs on our cold hands in winter. The Congregational Church is about as WASPy as it gets. Do some research and you will see references to the Pilgrims, the Massachusetts Bay Colony, Plymouth, even the friggin' D.A.R.

There is a small town in what is now Ukraine, on what was once in the shifting boundary between the Soviet Union and Poland. In the first years of the twentieth century it was a shtetl—a shtetl in the Pale of Settlement that surely made the villagers easy targets for pogroms. From the photos I could find, the streets were not paved, more like dirt lanes packed hard by carts and horses. There were stone buildings, no taller than two or three stories, some with thatched roofs. Women wore shapeless long peasant clothes with babushkas covering their heads; men wore all black attire, many with full beards and caps. The largest building was a synagogue where a man who might have been my grandfather, Chaim Yechiel Mikhl Bick, was rabbi but there was also Rabbi Isaac Bick, head of the rabbinical court of law, so maybe it was him. Maybe *he* was my grandfather.

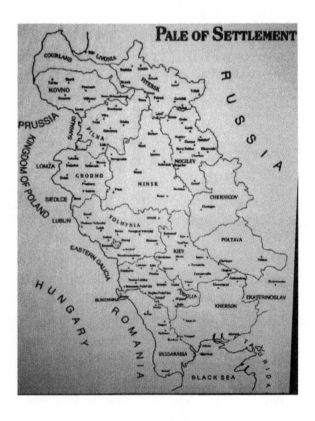

11

The Phone Call (1986)

SOME SERIOUS STRATEGIC PLANNING WENT INTO my weekly phone call to my mother. Fetch a crossword puzzle and pen. A glass of wine if it's after three, cup of tea if before. Comfortable place to sit. Clock in view. Then all I had to do was kick things off by saying, "Hey, mom. How are you?" For the remaining fifteen or twenty minutes—and believe me I timed it—all I had to do was say "Oh... " or "Hmmm"... or mostly "That's too bad"...and finally, "Well, I gotta go now." Sometimes I put the phone on speaker, set it on the counter and did my nails or paid my bills or made a pie. I promise you, she had no idea. We were both so well rehearsed we could have done our parts in a deep sleep. But this call was different. The phone was nearly back in its cradle when she said, "Oh, I told you I'm going to New York, right?" "You did not," I said, knocked slightly off balance by this change in our routine. New York is my hometown but my mother had, by that time, lived in San Francisco for over twenty years. As far as I knew she had not been back and had no remaining ties. As far as *I* knew. "Just for fun?" I said. "Well," she said, "You know my sister Millie, she's not doing so well, I've been really worried about her and, you know, she's so much older than me, and well, she was really more like a mother to me, so…" What the flying fuck! No, I do *not* know your sister Millie, you lunatic! I've never *heard* of this Millie person and what the holy hell are you talking about!

I don't know how old you are when you first understand the concept of relatives. Most of you probably grew up not even needing to understand it—it's just a given. That's my mom, that's my dad, that's my grandmother, that's my annoying cousin, Stewart. So, I don't really know how old I was or how many times I tried but I do know that more than once I asked my mother if we had any relatives. If she had any brothers or sisters. What about my grandparents? Her answer: "I don't remember." And then she'd change the subject. I know it's hard to understand, why I didn't keep asking or challenge such a ridiculous contention. The thing is, you'd have to know my mother to know how useless that would have been. Mostly, though, it's how my family was. We people in hiding don't ask many questions. And we answer even fewer.

12

Visiting My Father, Part Two (1978)

I T'S KIND OF COOL HAVING A PARENT WHO LIVES
like a graduate student. The half duplex where my
father and his girlfriend live is crammed full of books
and record albums, most of them stored in stacks
of milk crates. Two bean bag chairs, a ratty futon,
and three Siamese cats. We sit at the chipped linoleum table and smoke cigarettes—me, my father, and
Martha. I have no idea what he and I talked about
on the ride here from the airport since I was still
working on syncing up the picture I had held for so
long with the man who threw his arms around me
so fiercely at the gate. But now I am here and we
have twenty plus years of catching up to do. We talk

about Martha's work as a chemist at some company in New Rochelle. We talk about tennis, his latest passion. There's a court just at the end of their street and he has a regular game four times a week. We talk about Seattle Slew winning the Triple Crown and about the jets that collided over Tenerife. I say "we talk" but mostly I follow along, I listen, I'm interested. There was a blackout in New York and the U.S. returned the Panama Canal to Panama. He's intrigued by this new computer that Apple is making and is against the Trans Alaska Pipeline. And of course Elvis had died—we have to talk about that before it's time for me to head back to the airport.

On the way to JFK I'm thinking cool, I get to be smart and hip and unconcerned about social convention, that's who we are, me and my father. We're not like the rest of the world out there. My father and me, we're so alike. I knew it I knew it I knew it. All along, I knew it.

And then there was the flight home. Anyone who's ever gone through a trauma or been in shock can understand how I felt—so separated from my physical body, my senses muffled and dulled. "What?" I said, when the flight attendant asked if I'd like something to drink. "I'm sorry, what?" I said, after she repeated the question. All sounds and all sensations were somehow telescoped in the distance. Something was very wrong. Maybe the flu, maybe fatigue, maybe all the excitement. It was only my body I was feeling, nothing in my head or my mind or my heart. Only my body. It's obvious to you, I'm sure. And of course now I see that poor, deluded girl and think, honey, how could you be so out of touch, so naïve, so callow, and so sadly in need.

13

Dear Daddy (around 1959)

Dear Daddy,

I recieved your letter and I am willing to make a proposition with you. If you write me backs and tell me that you want to forget that you ever knew me I will be all too happy to try and forget about you. No — I shouldn't say that I willnot be happy to because you must admit that it will be quite hard for me to forget my own father even if my father wants to forget me.

I know that by writing this letter I am only reminding you of a life that you hated and I am very sorry for that. You have my word — if you want it — that you will never see or hear from me again. I cannot promise this for the rest of the "family" but I can promise it for myself. I can also assure you that I shall not send you any more gifts and if that is the way you want it you must not send me any. I have a feeling that it will be easier for you to forget that way.

In reading over this letter I realize that when you read it you will most likely think that I am trying to make you feel sorry for me. I can only tell you that this is not true. The words just seem to flow from my pen. — I am truley sorry if I upset you.
                    Goodbye,
            all my love, Liz

14

College (1965 to 1969)

<u>September, 1965</u>: I'm dropped off at the freshman dorm at George Washington University in D.C. Right on the sidewalk. I'll take it from here, mom. I chose this school because it was on the way to North Carolina where my boyfriend went to college and because I didn't get into Duke. D.C. was close enough to him, far enough from home. It's a city, sure, I'll go there. Why not?

<u>November 27, 1965</u>: Tens of thousands of Vietnam War protesters picket the White House, then march on to encamp at the Washington Monument…

...and me, I'm pledging a sorority, Delta Gamma, I believe, but I could be wrong and I kind of recall pretending to give a shit.

June, 1966: Civil rights activist James Meredith is shot and killed...

...and me, I'm setting off for a month with my boyfriend to the Outer Banks of North Carolina, then heading back to D.C. to find some parties to go to before school starts in the fall.

August 13, 1966: The National Organization for Women is founded in Washington, D.C....

...and me, I'm going to all the sorority and fraternity mixers held before school starts where I meet R., the guy who will be my first husband. We dance and drink and party and I teach him to smoke. There is no daylight between boyfriends for me, starting when I was fourteen. I am still technically dating my other boyfriend when I meet R. Hold on to one lifesaver until you know you have another to grab on to, that's how I did it.

October 15, 1966: Bobby Seale and Huey Newton establish the Black Panther Party...

...and me, I'm making use of all those cocktail dresses

I brought with me and sneaking into parties at Blair House or the French Embassy in Georgetown.

June 5, 1967: The Six-Day War begins. Israel occupies the West Bank, Gaza Strip, Sinai Peninsula, and the Golan Heights after defeating its Arab neighbors...

...and me, I'm sitting in the office of the Dean of Students who calls me in and says, *Liz, it's time to get serious. Look at all these Cs and you haven't declared a major. What do you want to do with your life?* I want to keep on going to parties, the embassy kind or the parties at frat houses where everyone brings a bottle of some rot gut crap and pours it all into a plastic barrel. How I chose my classes: the ones that didn't meet before 11 A.M. Even so, I still have to drag my bleary-eyed ass to class without ever having cracked a book, maybe never having purchased the book to begin with. High school all over again. Fucking lucky, is what I am, getting Cs. Give me till next semester, I say to the Dean. I'll figure something out.

January 30, 1968: The Tet Offensive begins followed six weeks later by the My Lai Massacre where American troops kill scores of civilians...

...and me, I'm watching slides in Art History classes. I had the most credits in Art History—more than

Philosophy or Anthro or French or Psych—so okay, Art History is my major. Fine, why not.

<u>April 4, 1968</u>: Martin Luther King is shot dead followed by five days of race riots. The White House dispatches some 13,600 federal troops. Marines mount machine guns on the steps of the Capitol and Army troops guard the White House. 1,200 buildings are burned. The occupation of Washington is the largest of any American city since the Civil War...

...and me, I'm crying because it's spring break, all my friends left for Paradise Island, Nassau before me and now the phones are down, the airport is closed, the city is on fire, and I am stuck here alone. Shit, spring break and nothing to do.

<u>May 12, 1968</u>: Over 2,500 activists from Mississippi arrive by bus in Washington, D.C. for a mass protest securing five acres around the Reflecting Pool in Washington to build a small independent city with its own stores, hospital, and city hall. This town of protest is known as Resurrection City and is an integral part of the Poor People's Campaign for civil rights...

...and me, I'm feeling single and attracting attention after being named Homecoming Queen so I'm on the lookout since R. graduates a year before me and leaves for an out-of-state job. That makes me single, right?

<u>June 5, 1968</u>: Robert F. Kennedy is shot by Sirhan Sirhan and dies the next day. Three days later, James Earl Ray is arrested for the assassination of Martin Luther King...

...and me, I'm packing for a three-month trip to Europe with a girlfriend. Since I can't imagine how it would have worked otherwise, my mother must have paid for the whole thing.

<u>August 22 to 30, 1968</u>: Police clash with anti-war protesters in Chicago outside the Democratic National Convention...

...and me, I'm going to conversion classes since R. is Catholic and we're getting married and I need to act like I give a shit.

<u>April 23, 1969</u>: Close to forty members of my school's chapter of the Students for a Democratic Society (SDS) seize control of Maury Hall and make multiple demands including an end to the Institute for Sino-Soviet Studies, an end to ROTC and military recruiting on the GW campus, and open admission into the George Washington University for all black students. The incident sparks nearly two months of campus unrest, reflecting the charged political atmosphere of Washington, D.C. during this time...

...and me, I'm walking my mini-skirted self to Lisner Auditorium past armored tanks and National Guard troops with, no shit, real machine guns on every campus block to meet the Four Tops because I am in charge of the spring concert.

June 28, 1969: The Stonewall riots in New York City mark the start of the modern gay rights movement in the U.S....

...and me, I'm getting married for the first time.

15

Paper (2005)

ON THE NIGHT BEFORE THE DAY MY MOTHER died I didn't sleep. After she'd dozed off or slipped into unconsciousness or partially died or whatever it was, that state she was in, I walked back from the hospital to spend the night at her place. I could practically stand in one spot and touch the four walls of this, her last sad home. She had left this room the way everyone has and the way everyone will leave here. Once you get to a place like this, you can forget about the future. She'd only lived there a few months but already her place was overrun by paper. She had file cabinets full of papers, cardboards boxes of papers, grocery bags stuffed with paper, stacks of paper on every flat surface. There was so much paper you barely noticed the safety rails and help-me-I've-fallen buttons and the kitchen with the mini-fridge and Easy-Bake Oven. Maybe that was the point. Or maybe holding on to paper felt like holding on to evidence of a life. But if you ask me it was another in her very impressive repertoire of indirect ways to communicate. Here's what I mean: I opened a file folder marked "Important Papers." In that folder I found the deed to her house three houses ago, a contract from her health insurance company (no longer valid), and a copy of the title for her dead husband's car that was sold, let's see, about fifteen years earlier. *Really, mom?* The file marked "Receipts" could barely hold its contents. Receipts from Macy's and Safeway and Nordstrom. From Pacific Gas & Electric and Golden Dragon Dim Sum and AT&T and 7-Eleven. Bus tickets and movie tickets and dry cleaner receipts.

All that paper, all that nonsense? I know what she's saying. She's saying: *You can't get rid of me that fast, missy. You're going to have to stay with me detail by detail. Bit by bit. Scrap by scrap.* It's not like demanding attention was anything new. Au contraire. Still, a funny thing to say by a woman who withheld from my sister and me even the tiniest details of her history. Including her date of birth.

So, in the middle of the night, while she was still alive but already too dead to question, after I'd emptied the file cabinet of all its folders and after I'd taken trash bag after trash bag after trash bag to recycling and after I'd sat on the bed and sorted and organized and put things into piles around the room, after all that, I swept my hand around the dark inside of the file cabinet just to be sure. Whether they'd fallen out of a now gone folder that should have been labeled THIS TIME I MEAN IT THIS IS IMPORTANT AND I'M NOT KIDDING GODDAMMIT! or hidden there on purpose so that only the Goodwill people or the most insanely compulsive freak would find them, there's of course no way to know. But there they were: those three love letters and that damn photograph.

16

Under My Bed (2005 to present)

B Y NOW, MY KIDS ARE TIRED OF BEING REMINDED about the fireproof box under my bed—*I know, I know, mom!* Every time I take a trip and then again if it's been awhile I remind them about the box, where it is and what's in it:

The names, addresses, and telephone numbers for my attorney, my financial advisor, my insurance agent, my CPA, and my closest friends

My will

A detailed Advance Health Directive

A copy of my driver's license

Account numbers and contact information for all financial holdings

Credit card numbers

A list of all pin codes and passwords

Information on my mortgage

Pre-paid arrangements for my cremation

My passport

Appraisal for a string of pearls

Long Term Care Insurance policy

The title to my car

Valuable coins and silver certificate bills

Two small gold ingots

My wedding ring

My birth certificate

Eight 100-dollar bills

17

The Age Thing

I NEVER, EVER, EVER LIE ABOUT MY AGE. WANNA know why? That last night, after I'd taken maybe a zillion trips to the dumpster and foraged my way through the mountains of crap in my mother's apartment, I found an unmarked grocery bag on the floor of her closet, about halfway down into the truly, utterly junk. Inside was a copy of her will. Her goddamn current, valid will. There she is, half a mile away, dying, and can't I just have my sorrow? Must you infuriate me, woman! And then in the same unmarked grocery bag, a file folder labeled "Misc" in which I found what turned out to be an active life insurance policy, which of course we knew nothing about. Here's the

Mr. Toad's Wild Ride I had to go on to figure that little issue out:

Me: Hello. I'm calling about a life insurance policy of my mother's, policy number xfg-27765-mg.

California: Date of birth?

Me: I've got her driver's license. It's 11/19/25.

California: That's not the date of birth I have listed.

Me: What do you have?

California: I can only give that information to the policy holder.

Me: But she's dead. My mother. That's why I'm calling.

California: Any other documents?

Me: Hold on… … …yeah, I've got her death certificate 11/19/27.

California: Nope. That's not it.

Me: Wait, wait 11/19/24, that's on her state id.

California: No.

Me: Can I guess?

California: I don't care. If you want.

Me: Well, how much is it for, the policy? What's it worth?

California: I can only release that information to the policy holder.

Me: Nevermind. I'll call back.

Me: Hello. I'm calling about a life insurance policy, my mother's. Policy number XFG-27765-MG. She's...

California: Date of birth?

Me: Ok, that's the thing. I have three different dates and I guess they're all wrong and the other lady wouldn't tell me.

California: Ok, no problem. We can do it another way.

Me: Oh good, thank you.

California: Just send us a copy of the birth certificate.

Me: There. Is. No. Birth. Certificate.

California: You'll just have to order one then.

Me: Look lady, I don't know the name of the town and I don't even think the country still exists, it was just this dinky little foreign place from the stone ages and I don't even know what her real name was… never mind. I'll call back.

Me: Hello. I'm calling about my mother's life insurance policy and before you ask, I don't have the right birth date and…

California: You can just fax the birth certificate.

Me: Look, I don't have anything like that and I can't get it. Can I just guess the date?

California: I guess.

Me: 11/19/18?

California: That's not what I have.

Me: 11/19/20?

California: Nope.

Me: 11/19/21?

California: No.

Me: Am I getting warm?… never mind, 11/19/22?

California: Yes, that's the date of birth we have in our records.

(And, yes, I ended up getting half her life insurance money but taking into account the number of hours I put into sorting through the shit I figure equaled to a reimbursement rate of about $1.25/hour.)

And one more age anecdote—not a frustrating, pull-your-hair-out kind of thing like the life insurance. More like another in the jaw-dropping experiences of what it was like to witness my mother in all her glory and another example of why I have been so neurotically honest about my age. Many years ago she came to Cleveland for a visit. I know that I was 30 years old because of this: I wanted my friend, Bridget, to meet my mother and vice versa so we arranged a lunch date. Not long into the conversation my mother says, "Bridget, you're so pretty. How old are you?" And Bridget—also someone who never lies about her age—said that she was 40, ten years older than I. Straight-faced and shamelessly, my mother says, "Amazing, me too!"

Amazing? I'll say! Bridget and I looked at each other, mostly gobsmacked by the ballsiness, knowing there was just no point asking the obvious: Do you know you said that out loud, mom? Do you remember that I'm in the room? And do you know that I can add and subtract? Really, mom? Amazing!

So, my age thing is like that fireproof box under my bed: another in the long line of examples of how to be NOT like that.

18

This Never Happened (1947 to 1957)

THE PIANO SITS TO THE LEFT JUST AT THE bottom of the three steps down into the sunken living room. A Knabe baby grand—matte black ebony, some of the gold leaf lettering flaked away, some of the ivory keys chipped and stained. The floor is carpeted, wall-to-wall, the way people liked it back then, the way the people with money covered their floors, so the way we did, too. My father is playing Chopin's Nocturne Opus 9, No.1 in B-flat minor. I am under the piano lying on my stomach, head on folded arms. This is where we always are and this is what we are always doing. I wouldn't exactly call it a dark piece of music though B-flat minor is a dark key. Ebony piano in a wood paneled room in a house in the woods. A dark-haired man with black eyes playing music in a dark key. I lie here every day and never want to leave. We don't speak. He plays the piece again *and please, one more time.* If you close your eyes you are somewhere sad and beautiful.

19

One Day in the Woods (around 1961)

IN THE WOODS BEHIND OUR HOUSE I SIT ON THE lap of a neighbor man. I am in high school, or maybe junior high, and the man is older than my father probably is but I don't know because my father is gone. He has his hand under my shirt, on top of my very small breast. I know what he wants but I am unwilling. I say *No, I'm sorry, I'm so sorry, it's not you, it's me. Don't feel bad and please don't hate me.*

20

Donna & Me (1952 to 1965)

Donna and I met waiting for the bus the first day of kindergarten, she was standing there across our country road, leaning against the stone wall on her side, wearing a flowered dress, her unleashed collie dog staying right there next to her. We waved coyly at first but from then on we went home together every day after school, either her house or mine. We played with Ginny dolls and Madame Alexanders, laying their clothes out on her third floor landing. We were tormented and terrorized by her brother and his friends, but not as much as we wanted. We idolized her sister with her blonde hair and big breasts and eager boyfriends. We forced my little sister to watch us act out radio soap operas and ignored her the rest of the time. We ran through the woods with Prince, her dog. We put on plays and took turns being the star, letting other kids have only bit parts. We ate minute steaks with garlic powder after school, fixed by Ida, her live-in maid. We ran away together but even though we thought we'd made it to California we were only on the other side of my woods. We played tricks on the other girls on our street. We picked grapes in back of my house, smushed them in a jar, and got pretend drunk on pretend wine, sitting under the weeping willow. We spied on our parents and their friends and all the weird things they did. We hid behind overstuffed armchairs when her father came home drunk. We never talked about my father, not ever. We snuck cigarettes from my house and alcohol from hers. We collected movie magazines, pinned pictures on our walls, and did imitations of Marilyn Monroe for the guests at our parents' parties. We never told anyone where we were going except maybe Ida, but only if she asked. We drank the alcohol left in glasses after the grown-ups had passed out. We told each other about boys, what we did with them, and when we went all the way and never told anyone else. We took the car keys before we were allowed to drive, went over the state line with fake IDs, and carved our initials in the wood at Maxl's bar, drinking whiskey sours and smoking Lucky Strikes. We were never without boyfriends. We flirted dangerously with repairmen. We never told our parents anything. We created our selves from our bond, constructed not only from love but from deep need. We grew each other up. We saved each other's lives, is what we did.

21

Millie (1992)

REMIND ME HOW THAT ALL HAPPENED," I SAID TO my sister. "How did you find her, I know it wasn't from mom. And where was I, anyway?" She couldn't remember the details either but somehow she found Millie. Our mother's sister, Millie. Found her living in some kasha-scented apartment in Queens or Staten Island, maybe Brooklyn, the old Brooklyn. Millie, the sister who was so much older than my mother, the one whose name was so casually dropped in the middle of a boring, predictable everyday phone call like I had known her all my life.

My sister and her husband flew across country to meet this aunt of ours. Even if they'd have asked me to go, which I'm pretty sure they didn't, I wouldn't have gone. I didn't go. By this time we knew we were Jewish. It was known and acknowledged. Sort of. But I can't for the life of me tell you how that happened. It's not like there was ever a conversation about it. Never a coming clean, *Let me tell you the whole story, kids.* It was more like a gradual, unacknowledged dawning; a process that happened slowly and unremarked upon, none of us ever having a direct conversation about the whole twisted charade. My sister was—continues to be—way out ahead of me in the embrace of our heritage. Both our parents contributed mightily to a legacy of shame in the form of self-directed anti-Semitism or some vague, non-specific opprobrium so I'm not going to take all of the blame for that. How could that *not* get passed down. After all, my mother and father each were completely cut off or disowned or some combination of the two by their entire families. The word Jew was not once ever uttered in our home. Not one time. Like the families of my friends we marched our floral print cotton-frocked selves to the Congregational Church on the hill for Easter, and Christmas at our house was an orgy of decoration, stockings, cookies left out for Santa, carols about Christ our Lord, all that shit. Couldn't be more Christian if ya tried.

Millie, apparently, did not know it was supposed to be a secret. There she was living her rightful life in a home that I am sure had Shabbat candles and a Seder plate in the cupboard and jars of herring in cream in the refrigerator. At least that's what I imagine. I don't know because I didn't go. "She's so lovely, Liz," my sister said. "You really should meet her. She's so sweet and she really loved mom." I did not go and I did not want to meet her and now, when I am ready and craving, it's too late because yes, she was so much older than mom so of course, now, she is dead.

Even today if I imagine what that reunion would have been like I can feel the contraction that comes with guarding myself. And as lovely as I am sure Millie was, I believe this: she would have painted some rosy picture. She would have made flimsy excuses about why she never tried to see us. She would not have given me a candid picture of her parents, my grandparents. She wouldn't have told me the truth about my mother. She would have judged me for not being Jewish enough, for coming to it too late, and being too assimilated, for not embracing it the way my sister had, marrying a Jew and all. Even if she *was* sweet and kind and lovely and my aunt, which I believe she was. She would just be some random old lady that I would feel no kinship to. I wouldn't love her. She wouldn't love me. And it would have been way too late for her to take me on to her wide lap and hold her hand to my wet cheek.

22

My Mother's Resume

MY MOTHER WAS AMAZING. NO TYPICAL FIF-
TIES housewife, she. She was a professional
photographer, a writer, a fashion designer, a jewelry
maker, a newspaper columnist, an interior decorator, a
boutique owner, and likely several other things as well.
She was positively driven by creative energy. She tried
so many ways to channel it but—like some tragedy of
Shakespearean proportion—her fatal flaws sabotaged
her at every turn. Alongside her raw creative energy was
a boundless need for acclaim and praise and stardom.
All of her real and true gifts were not enough. She had
to elaborate and embellish and flat-out lie. So how
would I know, for example, if that signed photograph

of Tennessee Williams she had hanging on her den wall was really a portrait she took as she claimed.

I don't think my sister agrees with me on this, but I'm not even sure she graduated from high school. She certainly was smart, likely self-educated, high school or no. But never one single reference to high school and certainly not to college. So this resume, with the education she brazenly and bogusly claims, is surely riddled with other exaggerations, to put it kindly.

(Ms.) LEE NELSON
5000 San Jose Blvd. - #108
Jacksonville, Florida 32207
904 - 731-2976

EDUCATION   Ecole D'humanité - Bachelor of Liberal Studies
Columbia University - Art Students League

PROFESSIONAL EXPERIENCE

ROSENBLUM'S, Jacksonville, Florida
General Merchandise Manager - Four fine specialty stores - sportswear, coats, dresses, gowns, furs, accessories - medium to couture.

Duties: Buying, merchandising, operations, personnel, branches, advertising, promotion, display.

FILENE'S, Boston, Massachusetts
Fashion Coordinator and Director of eleven stores

Duties: Merchandise development, fashion image, promotion, advertising, creating new departments, Executive Training Program, Christmas catalog, shopping and developing markets domestic and abroad.

Recommended to Filene's by Mr. Harold Krensky, hired by and reported to Mr. Richard Shapiro, Chairman of the Board.

FLAIR, INC., Westport, Connecticut
Owner-Manager

Duties: Flair was a miniature Bendel's--boots to bridals--a complete line of ready-to-wear, accessories, gifts, antiques and antique jewelry. Did all my own buying, domestic and abroad, ran a custom workshop featuring my own originals and created my own advertising and promotion - volume: about $1/2 million.

LEE NELSON ORIGINALS, Weston, Connecticut
Designed and manufactured small collections for Neiman-Marcus, Bronzini, Lord & Taylor, Hattie Carnegie, Lilly Daché, etc.

Interior Designer - many homes in Fairfield County.
Writer - Radio, television, short stories, advertising and promotion.
Produced, directed and commentated about 500 fashion shows.
Lectured on Fashion and Design at schools and Women's Clubs.
Made numerous television appearances as special guest--Home Show, June Havoc Show, Morning Show, etc. and many radio interviews.
Clients I have designed clothes for and "dressed": Mesdames Paul Newman, William Snaith, Harry Reasoner, Jack Klugman, Douglas Edwards, Robert Kintner, Abe Fortas, Herbert Salzman, Miss June Havoc, etc.

CIVIC ACTIVITIES

Promotion Director of Westport Chamber of Commerce
Chairman of the Connecticut Committee for "Care"
Hospitality and Fund Raising Chairman for the International Center of New York
Promotion and fund-raising for the United Nations Committee

REFERENCES

Richard Shapiro, Corporate Pres. of Gimbel Bros. and Saks Fifth Avenue, N.Y.C.
John Fraser, Jr. V.P., Executive Personnel Director of Allied Department Stores, N.Y.C.
Harold Krensky - President, Federated Department Stores

23

Once My Father Loved My Mother, Letter #1 (19—?)

Friday night—like I told you

Darling—

Some day—when I have plenty of time, and have grown more or less accustomed to being in love with you—I'll see if I can't put into words the way I feel about you. Right now it's impossible to do justice to the subject. You have to be outside an idea in order to comprehend it and define it and I'm right in the middle of this one and don't want to be bothered. Just let me sit here in the middle of a fleecy pink cloud, and mutter over and over to myself, "Whist, man! You're in love with her!" And, out of the corner of one eye, watch myself go on in the same routine I followed before I met you, just as if the world had not changed all around, all at once.

Cooper and I had a sort of philosophical discussion about me this afternoon, how while I didn't tell him yet how <u>soon</u> we're going to be married, he does know we intend to be. So now—I think it only fair to you that you and Cooper have a little talk sometime, alone, and you let him tell you all my faults. I have tried to, and have tried to be unequivocal about them, but I am unqualified to be a really good witness against myself, being more or less interested. Cooper, however, knows my every failing—sometimes, I think, all too well, but no matter—and will be able to give you a really clear picture of the bad things in me which would otherwise take a long time to find out. I do hope that there will also prove to be some <u>good</u> things, which will be revealed with time, but am pessimistic about the chances. Whatever good there is in me floats on the surface like a lily pad; the slimy growths are under water. But, anyway, I think you ought to have the benefit of Mr. Cooper's witness, because he has a splendid understanding, and perhaps what he can tell you will prompt you to fortify yourself against the tribulations to come. Never—oh! Never—to doubt or reconsider—at least I hope not, I pray not—in fact,

I'd be much disappointed in my judgment of you if it did cause you to doubt or recantation. You see where I am, now, darling?—at the selfish stage, where I unhesitatingly ask you to bear the worst in me—not in order to prove how strong and constant you are, but because I can't bear to be without you, and would inflict anything on you, in the way of my own faults, just so we could be together. But of course, my darling, you understand I'm joking, and that I recognize my faults, and want—now for the first time—to do what I can, for your sake, to fight them, and that I'll need your help in this fight. What kind of help?—Oh, just being yourself as I know you now—understanding, more or less tolerant, a bit flip, even tart, and loving— above all, loving. I think with that help I could even break the cigarette habit!

Well, anyway—down to a pack a day.

Darling, I love you and I'm running out of paper and I should get back to the store, and—well—will you pardon me while I buy a pack of cigarettes?

All my love,

August

24

Once My Father Loved My Mother, Letter #2 (19—?)

Monday night, December 16

Bienaimee,

I was heartbroken today to find the place had been rented. Being the first acceptable one I'd found, there had already been fixed a picture in my mind of our life in that frame, the walls and windows so, the doors here, and just such a distance and shading of sound between me and several composite and intensely jealous guests, in the living room, and you sweating over the kitchen stove, or perhaps cutting wood. The walls, just those walls, were lined with book-cases, chairs, pictures, vases and bottles of gin in a series of arrangements that faded into each other in a procession that moved like an andante. Each was different than the other, bearing only the relation that all were, separately, the ultimate, perfect and complete. Thus, I felt, would be the scene when we had passed through the seventh gate, parted the seventh veil. Why, paradise itself needed no better furnishing than this!

And now I have to go back to the old image, with the evanescent frame, with the walls shifting and moving, melting into each other, now rushing in and glaring at each other, now relaxing, receding, leaning back placidly to great spaces between, where I peer intently across a wilderness of rugs and tables and boxes, looking for a little moving speck in the distance, and shouting, "Hey, darling! Over this way!"

But strangely any way I think of it, it's still paradise; never has there been a scene like this; that chair over there: it's a chair apart; whether it's brown or green or yellow or blue, or whether new and shiny or shabby and old (and it has variously been all of these, and more), it is a chair that has been sanctified with something more than chairdom. It is not just to sit on, to serve a utilitarian purpose, or to grace a room, although it does these things. It has, indeed, a purpose, but a higher, and an older, one. You can see "Reserved for something better" written across every stitch of it, and when it was made, when the finishing touches were put on it, somewhere at hand were a couple of errant cherubs, checking it carefully against their notebooks of instructions, peering carefully at every detail. Presently they murmur, like silver bells tinkling, "Yes, this is it; this is the one we seek!" And they touch it lightly with star-tipped wands, and whisper themselves away into mist, while the chair has become, all in a moment, the solidest, intentest, most purposeful-looking chair that was ever built, or in all probability ever will.

Yes, it will be so. I can feel it. There will be an aura over everything about us. A romantic aura that breathes of love and passion, of the agony of tenderness, of days and nights together, and the mystic welding of two hearts and souls into a palpable vision of happiness with wings that span the universe; an aura sweet and overpowering, an overtone of rapture and mystical harmony. An aura percurable [sic], both transcendent and tangible; only to be dispelled, no doubt, by the smell of eggs burning in the frying pan. For Christ's sake, close that kitchen door.

So now we have to hunt some more. Sunday I'll have a list of prospective paradises, and you and I will make the rounds. On Sunday Milton is taking part in a skit of some sort, and wants us to be there. I'd like to go; I want to go. But I shall call Milton and say, "Milton, I may not be able to make it," or rather, "Milton, <u>we</u> may not be able to make it.

Milton, old boy," I shall say, "We are going—ahem—apartment hunting."

Just so be it with you and aimed at our marriage, there's nothing I'd rather be doing than.

I love you. Honest.

Augie

25

The Maginot Line (1963)

I THINK THERE MUST BE AN INTERNAL MAGINOT Line where our buried truths come up against the concrete fortification that is our defense and denial. At least that's what it feels like to me. I have very few distinct memories from my childhood, a handful only, the rest are hazy impressions or received text from other sources, another way my slate is blank. I can put a pin in a few times in my first decades where the battle at that line was palpable. This is one: I'm sitting in my car in the parking lot of my high school with my friend, whoever that was. We must have been talking about boys since that was the only subject I had the least interest in. She was asking me about my boyfriend, Larry, who was already away at college and in the middle of it all she said, "Does he care? About the difference, I mean?" I still remember the flushy, palpitating feelings, the slam up against that concrete wall, leaving me numbed with a buzzy anesthesia. It's that very strange experience of knowing something and not knowing it at the same time. A braver person would unclench, shake it off, and look straight at her and say, "I'm confused. What are you talking about?" A braver person would push through the barrier and let any and all information rise to the conscious surface. The truth is welcome here. But me, I wasn't that girl. Even though I knew there was treasure to be mined, I am quite sure I looked away from her, said "No," and quickly changed the subject. Being defended can feel strong because it's all about bricks and concrete and steel doors. But it's a posture that's built on fear and that makes you a big, giant wimp and I'm talking to myself now. Me, coward and co-conspirator, keeping up the family tradition, next in line to keep the slate blank.

26

Ladybug

I TOOK VERY LITTLE FROM MY MOTHER'S HOME after her death. You'd think there might have been some clothes, her having worked as a designer and in the rag business all those years. But, in the last decade of her life something weird was happening in her wardrobe. For example, she started wearing navy blazers with gold braid crests on the breast pocket, a kind of nautical look, very weird indeed. She used to have antiques, real ones. Chippendale chairs, Chinoiserie vases, Queen Anne settees, things they auction at Christie's, but who knows where all that went. At the end, there was cheap laminate furniture purchased for the move into her last, sad assisted living apartment—nobody wanted any of that. And there were boxes of jewelry that she had designed and made during that particular creative foray, all made of semi-precious stones, not a one of which I could force myself to like even a little bit. I *did* take one water-color of the San Francisco Bay that has her signature but which I am fairly certain she did *not* paint. I had asked her to save the small cast iron skillet she had used since I was a kid, perfectly seasoned over half a century of scrambled eggs cooked in butter. She either threw that away or gave it to someone else. So what I took were papers: a few letters, a file folder of photographs, and a big box of her writing, so much writing. What I have always told people—because it is what I was told myself—is that in her early days she wrote for the TV dramas like *Playhouse 90* and *Kraft Television Theater*, even writing an episode for the early *Twilight Zone*. None of those scripts were in the box, however. What I have are a six-hundred-page novel (unpublished), dozens of newspaper columns, at least thirty short stories (unpublished), poetry, and countless notes with ideas for future projects. And one more thing: a very small memo pad in the shape of a ladybug. On each ladybug-shaped page she had written one note:

We had water damage that ruined our carpets—we have every kind of insurance known to man—we were not covered for this particular kind of damage.

I gave some articles to the editor of the Examiner 6 months ago—she promised to get back to me in a week—not only has she forgotten me, she's misplaced the articles—and frankly isn't interested enough to read a duplicate set.

I invite a couple I want to impress for dinner and break one of my good wine glasses—which leaves only three—how do you serve 4 people with 3 wine glasses?

Three o'clock in the morning is a very lonely time.

I get on a bus and find I have only 40 cents and the fare is 60—and the bus driver makes me get off the bus.

Bob has bought me 3 pieces of good jewelry since we've been married and all 3 have been stolen.

When you can't sleep—and sleeping is something I don't get much of—at least not during the time when most people sleep—then at 7 or 8 in the evening when most people are getting ready to start the evening—I'm pinching myself to stay awake.

I think I have a daughter in Cleveland—but I'm not really sure—sometimes I think I just dreamed her up and that she really doesn't exist. I think I also have 2 grandchildren—but they too may be only figments of my imagination.

Right now—I need a friend desperately—someone who will listen and understand these silly, frightening, ridiculous, frustrating—sometimes disparate [or desperate] things that comprise my life.

I have another daughter whom I would like to talk to someday—like a friend.

This life that drags on and on and yet goes so quickly and some day soon it will be gone—and all that will be left are memories of broken glasses and broken dreams.

Bob has been waiting for 2 years for Tommy Ryan's company to get going so he could do a conference for them—the company has finally made it—they hired somebody else to do the conference.

When the samples came through they were totally useless. So here we go again.

I picked this silly pad to write upon because if I don't laugh about this I'll never stop crying.

27

I Hate San Francisco

THE FIRST TIME I WAS IN SAN FRANCISCO WAS for my mother's wedding—her third wedding— back in the mid-'70s. I was already a married woman with two small children of my own and she was having a wedding with bridesmaids. Yup, bridesmaids. And a bridal shower. With games. I mean, come on. That was one weird trip. The ceremony was at the giant redwood grove near the Russian River owned by the Bohemian Club, of which my stepfather-to-be was a member, and since he was a member he was allowed to escort women onto their sacrosanct ground. We had grown up surrounded by East Coast bleeding-heart liberals and my mother was tying her lot to this whole new thing. In its founding days, The Bohemian Club may have attracted artistic types but soon after it became an enclave for power-wielding, mostly Republican, mucky-mucks like Richard Nixon and Ronald Reagan. The Manhattan Project meeting took place there. Need I say more? Like I said, it was very, very weird.

So I really didn't have time to develop a hatred for San Francisco during that visit, more like a deep discomfort. The hatred started on the next visit when I brought my children. My mother and her new husband said they wanted to take us to dinner because *Nowhere in the world are there better restaurants than in San Francisco and we've been everywhere, everywhere!* We got dressed up and drove to what was indeed a fancy restaurant. The maître d' motioned us to follow when my mother said, "Smoking table, please."

He said, "I'm sorry, Ma'am, but we have no tables available in the smoking section."

And my mother scanned the restaurant, pointed to a table near the window and said, "What about that table?"

"I'm sorry," he said, "That is not in the smoking section."

"Or that one," she said.

"I'm sorry, Ma'am, we have no tables available in the smoking section."

She raised her voice and threatened that she would never come to this restaurant again, the thought of which probably made that guy's day. Then, as if she was doing him a big favor, she agreed to eat there anyway and we were led to a table in the non-smoking section. My two very young children were uncharacteristically quiet, probably confused about what this whole public hissy fit was about. I, of course, was mortified, trying to silently apologize to all the other patrons who couldn't hide their disdain. Then, to top it off, our waiter arrived to take our drink orders and my mother said, "Please bring me an ashtray."

Her brazenness was a thing to behold. I wish I had just a smidgen of the chutzpah this woman had but in situations like this, well, I was beet-faced embarrassed. What followed was a predictable back and forth that involves him saying it's a non-smoking table and her saying that she smokes, she has rights, and she would like an ashtray and him saying he's sorry but that's impossible and her getting louder and more insistent and him apologizing again and her finally saying, "Do you know who I am?"

No, mother! He does not know who you are. Nobody knows who you are, at least not in the way you mean it, not in the way you hunger.

My next visit I joined my mother and her husband on a house-hunting trip in the city since they had been living in his bachelor apartment. I'd never criticize my mother's real estate instincts, it's not that. She was smart and shrewd. But that trip riding in the cramped-up excuse for a back seat in a Fiat Spider, it's like I was a prisoner forced to witness something dreamt up by Edward Albee. Bickering does not do it justice. Belittling, debasing, disdain… followed by some passive (or passive aggressive) retort. Don't bother fighting, man. She'll get her way in the end, we both know that. EVERYONE KNOWS THAT!

The trip after was planned so I could attend the opening of a play my stepfather wrote, a play called, *Everyone's Favorite City*, by which he naturally meant San Francisco, so already I'm nervous. For weeks beforehand I heard all about how many famous people would be there, how they were sure it would be a long run, how they'd had such great pre-show buzz. I'm not sure I can paint a picture that does this justice. First, there were about six people in the audience and none of them were famous. Second, it was a musical with really, truly ridiculously awful music. The story was a circle-jerk exercise about how lucky they are to live in San Francisco, the city where every single soul in the whole wide world wants to live, that they were the lucky few, blah blah blah. Three of the six people in the audience left after about twenty minutes and I spent the rest of the time trying like hell to figure out what I could possibly say after it was finally, blessedly over. It was the apotheosis of pathetic.

* * *

On my next trip, I visited on my own. My plan was
to help around her apartment with things she couldn't
do, hadn't gotten around to, or hadn't noticed needed
doing. I'm cool with that. It was much easier to talk
while I was cleaning the oven or sorting through
massive piles of paper. She needed to go to the bank
and take care of some business but when we got there,
there was a long line. (Let me take a minute here to
say that the concept of a line never meant anything
to my mother. At worst, a line only made her charge
to the front a little less direct.) I held on to the sleeve
of her coat, trying to keep us in our proper place in
line but I was no match for that dame. She marched
up to the front of the line right past all the other
people like she owned the damn place, leaned close
to the window, and started talking to the teller. As
I exchanged conspiratorial looks up and down the
line, trying to silently say, *Yes, I know, she's a piece of
work, I'm so sorry*, the teller did her best to inform
my mother that there were other people ahead of
her, would she kindly return to the end of the line,
someone will be with you as soon as possible, all the
while my mother's voice was getting louder, more
insistent, more imperious, culminating in, "Do you
know who I am?"

Again, no, mom. No one knows who you are.

* * *

This wasn't the last time I witnessed my mother hurling that pseudo question at someone she felt had wronged her. But that question has been persistent: *Do you know who I am?* I do not, mother. I do not know who you are. You are a maddening mystery. And because it makes me feel just a little better to believe that you acted *not* intentionally, *not* maliciously but rather out of psychological myopia and sheer lack of insight, it's a good guess that *you* didn't know who you were either. You surely didn't know who *I* was. How could you? There was no room in there for another living soul.

Most people working in the field of child development concur: early bonding and the development of secure attachment is vital for nurturing a sense of safety and that an insecure attachment can inhibit emotional development, often leading to difficulties in forming relationships later in life. Dan Siegel, who is a leading expert in the field, talks about the importance of "the mother's gaze." He is being literal here. How an infant sees herself reflected in the loving gaze of her mother impacts how the infant grows to feel about herself and her place in the world. The mother's eyes act as a mirror, reflecting back a loving, safe, secure image for the child to absorb. I doubt my sister and I had that. Understand, I do believe that my mother loved me, at least to the extent that she was capable. But her own sucking need for validation was so strong, I highly doubt that her gaze provided us with a sense of security and self-worth. I often think of a line in the movie *Mother* when Debbie Reynolds tells her son, played by Albert Brooks, that she loves him. He patiently replies, "I know you think you do."

So, when I think about my mother's cringeworthy reproof—"Do you know who I am?"—now I hear it less as a rebuke and more as an actual question. I hear her asking this of herself in some kind of desperate effort to fill a bucket that clearly had a giant hole in it. And I hear it as a question I have been grappling with myself for decades, early on looking to others (read: men) to define me and only in my later years developing what I would call a reliable sense of myself. When you combine the parental pathology with the utter lack of information about family history, it's no mystery why that question would become a lifelong inquiry for me.

So, San Francisco is decidedly not my favorite city, even if they might have the best restaurants on planet Earth. I know that I can't claim legit PTSD, that would be way too princessy and too dismissive of all the people who have all the reason in the world to startle at a car backfiring. But when I'm there, as soon as the plane starts its descent, I start feeling it—the bracing, the carapace forming over my heart, all the ways I have felt smaller and undone and wishing mightily that I could be a better person.

28

Letter from My Father's Wife
after His Death (1997)

January 22, 1997

Dear Liz and Margaret,

I have made each of you a copy of my personal Gus scrapbook, which I put together in November to share with my family. , Yesterday I added a few items, not different in kind. It's certainly not complete; there's nothing about Union Carbide, where he worked for about ten years, or about his computers, or about many of the many other things that filled his life.

For you I pulled a small sample of the letters and financial stuff. All his canceled checks from 1960 to the present were there, as well as tax returns, etc, etc. when I began to sort through in November. If you ever want to see more, you're welcome. I'm keeping a large carton in the attic. As to the burning question of his financial support, he sent $290 every two weeks until 10/63. Then beginning in 4/64 he sent check of $200 and then $100, and then stopped after he left the Better Vision Institute in late 1966. Gus' list of checks is attached.

What does it mean? What light has been cast for me?

With credit to my shrink Lisa, whom I've been seeing every so often since Gus' heart attack in 1992, I offer a disease model explanation. The fact he thought seeing you was unbearably painful might have had some basis in the biochemistry of his own head, and in the secret history of his life.

- Gus surely was obsessive-compulsive. It made me crazy that he would not throw away cartons, jars, magazines, bags, and filled the refrigerator and freezer to bursting. And was totally insensitive to my tears, begging, or offers to institute inventory control, refusing to view the behavior as a problem.

- He experienced a major depression 5/85 to 5/86, which had been preceded, beginning in 1982 by short periods of deep melancholia. He was treated for hypothyroidism in 1987, and there were no episodes of depression after that, except one in 1994 that lasted 3 days.

- He certainly was severely depressed about 1970 when he was evicted from his apartment, and before that, based on the letters.

- Gus refused to speak to me during his 1985-86 depression,, and I have written communications from him (lost in the attic at the moment) with the flavor of those letters from the 60s, fearing financial disaster, threatening suicide, and blaming me for everything.

Lisa points out that his technique of walling off parts of his life saved him from whatever "homelessness would have meant for him", and enabled him to live to 80, and to have a life with many satisfactions. She also points out that I since I know virtually nothing of what he went through in his early life, I can't make judgment about his response to it.

She has always found the closed, secret quality of his personality very unusual about our marriage. She said early on that that one member of a couple may express feelings for both, and that I provided that to him. There is no doubt in my mind that he really, truly loved me. She said on my most recent visit in at this November that I may have been the one love of his life, which is certainly very sad

At this point I believe understanding is what is needed, not forgiveness. I think he did as well as he could, despite doing hurtful, callous and dreadful things with respect to you both.

I thank you for helping you come to closure in this difficult matter. I hope it may be of some good for you.

Sincerely,

Martha

29

The Scrapbook (1997)

I STILL HAVE THE BLACK AND WHITE PHOTOGRAPH of my father. I keep it in one of the boxes in my storage closet, along with other loose, random bits of nostalgia, though nostalgia implies *pleasant* and pleasant is not the feeling I have when I think about that picture. Rather than nostalgic, I'd say keeping the picture is superstitious. It seems vaguely dangerous to destroy every trace of a relative as significant as a parent. And it seems psychologically naïve too. You can't just *will* someone out of existence. You can't pretend the father you had was *not* your father. Wait, I take that back. You *can* do that. You can actually build a doppelgänger and slap on any quality that suits you. In fact, an absent father is a perfect canvas. You want the strong, silent type? Poof! You got it! You want the sensitive artist who's too pure for the madding crowd? No problemo! Or maybe it's the James Dean kind of rebel you want? You won't have to pay till later but you pay with interest and the price is pretty fucking high. And that's why I keep the picture.

The only thing I have left from my father *besides* that black and white photo is what I *guess* you'd call a scrapbook that was sent to me after he died by I *guess* who you'd call my stepmother. When I saw my father again after all those years, he was living with Martha, whom he would marry some years later. (Martha: I don't know if you are still out there somewhere and chances are you will never read this but, if you do, I apologize. You're probably not going to like hearing what I have to say about you.) Though, truth be told, between the two of them, Martha was a better deal. She was/is just a few years older than me, some kind of advanced degree in some kind of science and, what I can say now after my *own* advanced degree in psychology, a whack job. The technical term would most likely be Asperger's. She was oddly direct, strikingly devoid of emotion, and sort of appealing in a weird way. And she had some remarkable ability that I did not have. While I'm sure she must have been heartbroken and deeply challenged during much of their time together, she seemed to have a deep compassion and acceptance for the exceedingly flawed man she loved and married.

Even so, what she chose to include in this scrap-book she sent—one to me and an identical one to my sister—speaks volumes about them both. Here's a sampling of what she believed would be a remembrance of our father:

Page one: A receipt from cvs drugstore for a heating pad and deodorant

Page two: A query letter my father wrote soliciting some freelance work

Page three: A parking ticket from five years before

Page four: A summons for jury duty

Page five: A prescription for blood pressure medication

Page six: An arrest warrant for disorderly conduct

Page seven: A photograph of their cat

Page eight: Handwritten note about the last run of the Third Avenue El noting departure from Chatham Square station at 6:04 P.M.

Page nine: A copy of a Walt Whitman poem

Page ten: An application for membership in the Winged Foot Golf Club

Page eleven: Copy of a bill from Burke & McGlinn, attorneys, regarding a suit against the Town of Clarkstown

Page twelve: Copy of a page from the American Heritage Dictionary about the word "comprise"

Page thirteen: A newspaper article entitled, "What's Cooking in Virtual Kitchens"

Page fourteen: A copy of an invitation to a cocktail party

Page fifteen: A copy of a poem by William Dunbar entitled, "Lament for the Makers"

Page sixteen: A Shouts and Murmurs column from *The New Yorker* by Martin Amis called "Tennis Personalities"

Pages seventeen through the end: Other similarly weird, random shit

And tucked in the back, a series of letters between

my mother and father written sometime soon after their separation and two letters from me to him. But after reading two of the letters, I was so topped out by the glut of family psycho wackiness, I just couldn't take one more shred of pathology. The rest of that shit could wait.

30

That Motherfucking Black Coat (1989)

MY MOTHER CAME FOR A VISIT, FLYING FROM THE West Coast to Cleveland where I was living at the time and we went shopping, because—like I said—shopping was what we did because shopping was the only way to tolerate it. It was end of season, sale time, and I was in need of a winter coat. It was Cleveland, after all, a place where winter is brutal and a good winter coat is a mandatory item. I'm not the easiest person to please, so it felt like providence coming across a beautiful black coat, yummy cashmere, my size, and *hot damn!* half price. From every angle in the three-way mirror, it was the perfect coat. My mother says, "Let me buy that for you." Right away there's that inner clench but Smart Me manages to says, "That's very sweet but, no, I'll buy this myself." My mother says, "Please, Liz." She says, "It would mean so much to me." She says, "Truly it would make me happy." And then Dumb, Cheap, Greedy Me says, "Well, thank you, mom. That's lovely."

It's about seven steps to the cash register, so far so good. My mother hands her credit card to the clerk and we're still okay—but wait, she looks at the credit card slip and says, "Yeesh, *that's* the sale price!?" "Mom," I say. "Just let me buy it." She gives me a look, shakes her head, and, with pointedly obvious labor, signs her name. The coat is on its way into a shopping bag and my mother says, "Here, wait. Let me try it on."

Just to paint a picture, I am 5'7", my mother barely cracks five feet. I wear a size 8; she wears a size 2, maybe. You can hardly find her in all that yardage. "It's perfect," she says. "I love it." The saleswoman, my new best friend, offers to see if there is one in my mother's size, even calls to other stores in other states but this is the very last one in any size, anywhere on planet Earth. My mother says, "I've been looking everywhere for a black, cashmere coat." And here comes Stupid Me again saying, "For California? Really?"

There's the world where people say what they mean and then there's *this* world. To be fair, my mother *was* indeed saying what she meant—just not in actual words. In fact, if you ignore her words you can hear her more clearly: *I don't <u>really</u> want to buy you that coat.*

I don't want to buy it but I __do__ want credit for buying it. And besides, do I really want you to have something I can't have? But since I ignore what she is clearly, loudly, patently, obviously saying the dialogue continues:

Her: I really love this coat.

Me: Fine. You take the coat, mom.

Her: No, I said I would buy it for you… [pause]… even though it's just what I've been looking for. And anyway, it's way more expensive than anything I'd buy for myself.

Me: Mom, just take the damn coat. Here, *I'll* buy it for *you.*

Her: I want *you* to have it.

Me: (Sigh)… Well, okay, but I'm going to pay for it myself.

Her: Can't you do this one thing for me and let me buy it for you? You never let me do anything for you, Liz. Why don't you let me do anything for you?

Me: … [pause]… Okay. If you're absolutely sure… thank you.

In the car on the way home she tells me she really loves that coat, it's the perfect coat, and she really, really wants that coat. Me, I say nothing. I'm too busy thinking. *What if I just drove right over that embankment? Do I still have that cache of Valium in my medicine cabinet saved up for my fatal illness? How long do you have to hold down the pillow anyway? I'd qualify for the insanity defense, right?*

31

Before She Was Married,
My Mother Was Loved by a Man
Named Wally & Had a Chance for a
Different Life, Maybe the One She
Really Wanted (194—?)

P.O. Box 154
Auckland, N.Z.
24th November

Lee Dear:

By now it is all over. [What is over?] *November 15th was the day. Shimmering black chiffon draped over a lovely, soft skin, shimmering black chiffon trembling over the firm, pointed breasts, shimmering black chiffon lingering over a rounded thigh. Happy Birthday, Lee! Many, many happy returns of the day! And Ezra, where was he?* [Who is Ezra?] *I would have given my right arm to have been with you, to have had your eager eyes look into mine and smile. And Ezra, where was he?*

By now it is all over. The Fair is all over. [The New York World's Fair of 1939, maybe? Somehow I believe that's where my parents met.] *Perhaps even the anguish of the soul in which you wrote to me is over, all over. I sincerely hope so. I read so much in your letter, Lee. Much that was never imprisoned in a written word, so much that was written in the tears of your heart. With all my heart I hope that you have found some comfort, some peace.*

And now, I <u>*am*</u> *with you. Here! Take my hand, clasp it tight and don't be afraid. Little girls mustn't get scared so quickly. I've been here all the time but you didn't see me. I stretched out my hand to you that first time at the Fair* [So did she meet both my father and this man, Wally, at the Fair?], *because, in spite of your bold speech and imperious air, I knew you were afraid, shrinking, sensitive and I yearned to give you the hand clasp which would have told you I understood the inarticulate unhappiness of your soul. But you were afraid of me and the more I saw your fear, the tenderer my desire to soothe and to calm. For that I sought your lips, your arms, that your mental resistance should mix with your body. And melting, your spirit would have mingled with mine. Because, Lee my dear, I wanted to take from you too. In calming your fears, I should have dispelled my own, in making for you one moment of happiness, my own unhappy wandering would have ceased. Didn't you see my outstretched arm, Lee? Even as the train sped along the platform, tearing me away from you and Ezra* [Was Ezra really my father with another name?], *did you not see the pain in my smile, my hand outstretched?*

But now you hold my hand, tight, firm. You tell me of Ezra's selfishness, of his smugness and then ask me to explain his aloofness. Lee, my dear. Ezra is my friend and I love him. He is indeed selfish, he is indeed smug. But when he hurts you, he does not do it wittingly. He does it foolishly, unthinkingly. His faults are not more grievous than our own, his virtues are many and he is my friend. [So, is she in a relationship with two men who are close friends?] *I have worked with him for years, been with him continually, and I know that he is worthwhile. I begged him to write me regularly, frequently. He does not. I have asked him to do certain things—requests ignored. He is erratic, impulsive, carried away by something new—but he never forgets. Bear with him, Lee. He can be very fine. If he has made you unhappy I am sure he does not realise it. Please try to see him again and find out for yourself. He has told me nothing.* [About what?]

If you have not already done so, please take up your theatrical scholarship. [!! We never heard a thing about theatrical aspirations!!] *Don't you see, you must. Your father will continue to help you, even now, if he sees you are set on the stage and that it will make you happy. You talk about working as a matter of principle, but, surely, you realise deep down, that you are fooling yourself. You're afraid, that's what! Yes, Lee, afraid of the step, afraid that should you fail, nobody will understand. Don't be misled, don't be foolish. If you allow this desire, if it is all honest and deep desire, to be frustrated, the bitterness of it will haunt you through the years. A thousand times better to fail in a courageous bid. Go on, Lee. Go on!*

Alternatively, you may give your hand in marriage to the professor. [Who is the professor? Was this an epithet for my smarty-pants father… or someone else?] *And your pent-up urge for life, for expression, will be fulfilled in the glorious creation of babies, and you will be happy. Yes, that's it, perhaps, after all! Babies, Lee! Your maternal instinct has been thwarted and you have been dissatisfied, unhappy. Bigger and better babies for bigger and better bombs. Kiddies for the cannon, progeny for poison gas. That's right, Lee, don't*

take up the scholarship. Even if you have confidence you could make it, what message could you possibly hope to put across to your audiences? Have babies instead. The girls will be nurses and will drive army lorries dressed in natty uniforms and gas masks, the boys will wear tin hats and fire Bren guns and drop high explosive bombs on towns. Don't you read the complaints in the newspapers? This war's too tame. D'ya call this a war?
[So much sarcasm. So much prescience.]

Forgive me, Lee. I am bitter. I knew an England that burgeoned with green life in the bright, spring sunshine. I knew work and play, creation and joy, laughter and sunshine, and food and wine by a crackling fireside. England, my England. And now they seek to stain the fair, fresh fields with the tainted, dark blood of our poor, deceased humanity. And over the world scurry the hordes of refugees, barred, pushed on, sympathy without help, whilst others are tortured and murdered, and even left to live a life which offers nothing but death. Families uprooted, torn asunder, mutilated, mother from child, a woman from her man.

No, don't let go of my hand, Lee. I need <u>you</u> now.

May I ask a favor of you, Lee, please? Will you contact an American organization or organizations working for Peace, any organizations which have renounced War as a method of "settling" international disputes. I want them to send me any literature, posters, etc. they can. I am forming a branch of the Peace Pledge Union in Auckland, tough work and even becoming dangerous because of attacks from "patriots." If the organizations can't send the stuff directly, will you? Please?

Lee, dear, your promise to have English muffins with me in London makes me laugh and cry together. I swear it, Lee, morning coffee and muffins in London, in Piccadilly. Then we'll stroll Leicester Square and look at the statue of Shakespeare, along Regents Street, Oxford Street, Bond Street, Pall Mall. Lee, my dear, if you'll keep hold of my hand we'll cross the Channel to Paris, les Champs Elysées, café noir avec des croissant and des brioches, garcon [sic] *and we'll sit in the sunshine and watch the ceaseless stream of gay Parisians and we'll go to L'eglise du Sacre Coeur and lunch at La Coupole and go out to Fontainebleau and take our tea at that the-dausant* [sic] *in the Bois de Boulogne. For dinner we'll go to—but I forget, it may all be blown to bits by the marvelous machines and chemicals made by our great men of science.*

Come closer to me, Lee, because we both have been hurt, frightened and we can help one another. Closer, Lee, till I can see in your eyes a gown of shimmering black chiffon, draped over a lovely soft skin, trembling over soft, rounded breasts...

Valete,
Wally.

Bless you for the photograph. I love it so. I shall be able to talk to you now so close to my side, in the early morning, and in the still hours of the night.

32

A Bare-Bones Chronology

THIS IS NOT AN AUTOBIOGRAPHY. IT IS NOT A coherent, reliable story of a life. Members of my family—including my mother, my sister, and my two children—seem to have my same nearly empty cache, none of us able to call up more than a scant handful of memories from our childhoods. I don't know if it's more psychological—some pain blocking mechanism—or if it's just the way the brains are wired in this family. In any case, without a strong stable of memories to draw on it's not so easy to construct a coherent story. What I have instead is a chronicle of emotion and cathexis, skittering through different points of my life, attaching once in awhile to a specific memory but often not.

So here is a bare-bones chronology of the big events that form at least the skeleton of my life:

1947: I'm born in New York City; my sister follows five years later and we move to a bedroom community in Connecticut before she's a year old.

1953 to 1957: My father commutes to New York City to work in advertising and in the following years he is away from home more and more until probably in about 1957 when my parents tell me they are getting divorced—a conversation I can only guess happened but have no concrete memory of. In about 1957 we move to the house on Steep Hill Road, leaving the home we all loved.

1958ish: Shortly after my father leaves home for good he asks me to take the train into New York City to have lunch with him at which point he tells me that it's too painful for him to see me anymore and I will not see him again for nearly twenty years.

1963: At around age sixteen, I meet my first serious boyfriend, Larry, and he and I will be together for a few years until my freshman year in college.

1964ish: My mother remarries, a nice man, I guess. I am in high school, getting ready to go to college and about as disconnected from them as possible so he does not take up significant emotional space for me.

1965: I leave for college in Washington, D.C., graduate in June of 1969, and get married for the first time two weeks later.

1970ish: My mother's second husband dies.

1970 to 1974: My first husband gets jobs in two small towns in Ohio and then in Cleveland. I have no profession and no thoughts of a profession and so we go where he is sent. My two girls are born in 1972 and 1974.

1974ish: My mother moves to San Francisco, having met a man she will marry soon after.

1975: I am bored and depressed and finally enroll in graduate school. Four years later I get my PhD in psychology.

1978: My sister uses a private detective to find our father whom I have not seen or heard from since that lunch at Rockefeller Center. Shortly after, I fly to New York to see him.

1978: My father and his wife come to Cleveland with the plan to stay at our house on their way farther west. After less than an hour I ask him to leave. This is our final contact.

1980: I am divorced for the first time.

1981: In graduate school I meet the man who will become my second husband, a relationship that lasts about seven years.

1986: In an ordinary phone call my mother mentions a sister we never knew she had and we start to get information on our extended family.

1990: I get married yet again, uproot my entire life, move to Portland, Oregon. This liaison lasts about seven years.

1992ish: My sister and her husband visit our aunt Millie.

1996: My father dies.

1998: I meet my last love and we get married.

1998: My mother's last husband dies.

1999: My husband dies.

2001: My mother takes me and my sister and her family on a horrendous cruise.

2002: My mother visits me in Portland.

2005: My mother dies.

33

My Father's Favorite Poem,
One I'm Told He Recited Often

I think I could turn and live with
          animals, they're so placid and self-contained,
I stand and look at them and long.
They do not sweat and whine about their condition,
They do not lie awake in the dark and weep for their sins,
They do not make me sick discussing their duty to God,
Not one is dissatisfied, not one is demented with the
          midline-mania of owning things,
Not one kneels to another, nor to his kind that lived
          thousands of years ago,
Not one is respectable or unhappy over the earth.

—Walt Whitman, "Song of Myself"

34

My Sister's Wedding (1992)

Twenty-some-odd years ago, my sister married a Jew. There was a chuppah and a ketubah. They broke the glass, we hoisted them up on chairs, and we all danced the hora—mazel tov!

Twenty-some-odd years ago, the last of my stepfathers was still alive. He was a Republican, former navy man, member of the uber-conservative, fancy-schmancy Bohemian Club, and poster boy Protestant. What he made of this wedding, oy, who knows! I'm only 99.999% positive about this but I would bet the family farm that my mother never let him in on her background—our background—not in all the years they'd been married which at that point was over twenty. In other words, he had no idea he was married to a Jew. He was one of those people you could imagine had never actually *met* a Jew, at least knowingly. "Not that I have anything against them," he would probably say. "As a people," he would add. And he would still blindly adore her, of this I am sure—but with a certain bewilderment, maybe sort of like someone who discovers his house cat is actually an ocelot.

And what *must* it have been like for my mother at that wedding. An immigrant from a shtetl in Ukraine, daughter of a rabbi, descended, I have come to learn, from thirty-three generations of rabbis—in fact, traced back to King David, so the story goes. Here's her heritage, fully, proudly—and finally—acknowledged. Here is her tribe. And then there's her new life. She was swimming in the Junior League-y circle of WASPY matrons in San Francisco—museum docents, consular corps, Bohemian wives—ever insinuating herself into the fringes of the power elite, ever desperate to crack into the core. My poor mother. What a mind fuck.

My sister, though, seemed to have not a shred of resistance or even awkwardness. This display of ethnicity was not done to appease her new husband and his family, they all life-long, loud-and-proud Jews. She herself embraced it with a big giant bear hug. She was so much farther down the path than I back then—maybe still—and I remember a jumbled mix of respect, repulsion, and confusion in the presence of her unabashed embrace of her Jewishness. It hadn't been that long, after all, just a mere handful of years that we'd known this about ourselves. What eased her process or, more to the point, what got in the way of mine, I still do not quite understand.

35

Letter Between My Parents, #1
(1962)

4/2/62

Dear August

I will ask once again if you can possibly gather up enough emotional stability to see me. I do not use that phrase unkindly or critically. I believe you when you tell me the reasons you can't see me and the effect I have on you. It breaks my heart for your sake that after all this time you have not been able to find any peace within yourself.

I have concentrated every bit of strength I possess to try to build my business. It has been a Herculean effort. By all that's reasonable, I should have failed. I started without a penny investment but I have stuck it out—I don't know how but I have—against overwhelming odds. There is no need for you to keep on reminding me in every note that any day, any moment, any time you may lose your job—and my children will be left without support—that fear is ever with me. It does not help matters, believe me. I am just as anxious as you are to become self-supporting—to have some feeling of security for the children's sake. The business is the only way out. I am worth nothing on the job market. At best I can get a sales job for $50 a week. How far would that go in this day and age. You keep warning me not to make it any harder for you. I have tried to ask nothing of you. The one area that I have continued to need help from you has been support money. That we cannot do without. It will take at least another year at best before I can expect to draw any kind of salary from the business. Please, I beg of you—don't add the torture of financial insecurity— don't force me to go to bed every night wondering when the axe will fall—when my children will be homeless. If it should happen, we will face it—I don't know how— but until then, I need some peace of mind to concentrate on the business. I work 6 days a week. I get home after 6 o'clock and start cooking dinner. I do my cleaning and ironing at midnight. Day after day. I'm not asking for pity—just a little understanding. If I could see you, if I could explain certain things to you. If you could possibly face me without bitterness and resentment, we could help each other.

Believe me, I will not disturb you with things of the past. The past has served only one purpose—it has forced me to grow up—belatedly—but I have grown up. Every time I look at Liz I thank God she had you for a father—her sheer physical beauty, her keen analytical mind, her stark honesty—she has inherited all these from you—and I am grateful. Every time I hold Margaret in my arms I am convinced she would not be the same if she were not your daughter.

I have hurt you—I took your tenderest feelings and outraged them—but this I swear—never consciously, never with any intent to hurt you. It all stemmed from my own blindness—the blind darkness of the emotionally immature. It is only in retrospect that one can understand.

In my own stupid immature mind there was an idea this might happen and that is why I begged you to live alone for a little while—to give us a cooling off period—a time to catch our breath and grow-up a little. If you remember that was before, long before the final break-up. By the time that happened, emotions were too raw, too hurt, but perhaps if you had listened—taken a room at the Y for just a few weeks—you would have given me a chance to realize how much you meant to me. How much I felt your loss—how lightly I had valued your wonderful traits.

Liz graduates in June. You should see her. You would be so proud. She is so beautiful and truly lovely inside. She is disturbed, of course, but she has found her own areas of strength.

Little Margaret, she has been hit the hardest of all—you see how blind we can be—I had always worried about Liz and figured Margaret could take anything. Yet Liz has managed to come through and Margaret's life has been destroyed—I hope not permanently, but I'm deeply concerned about her. She refuses to accept the fact that you have left and I don't know quite how to handle the situation. It has affected her relationships with her friends and teachers.

I won't insist if you really feel you can't see me. I will understand—and this letter is not meant to upset you—that's the last thing in the world I would want to do now. I no longer feel noble and superior. I have looked into the deepest recesses of my being and I have shuddered in shame.

As ever—

Lee

36

Letter Between My Parents, #2
(1962)

5/27/62

Dear August:

I am enclosing the cancelled check you asked for.

As for Liz's graduation, you must follow your own conscience. If you cannot face coming, I do believe you should drop her a few words and make some excuse. Just ignoring her letter is an unnecessary cruelty. I know you do not wish to hurt her more than necessary. She still loves you very much and her image of you is still shining and untarnished. I would like to keep it that way, for her sake, as well as yours. Someday, you may be able to resume some relationship with your children. If that day comes, I do not want them to feel any anger or bitterness. It would also be nice if you sent her a graduation present. This is a pretty big day in her life—it's her first graduation.

As for the house situation, the last one fell through today. I waited too long and the house was sold. However, I am about to close on another one. It is a bit more costly than the first, but I believe a good investment and easily resalable.

I borrowed quite a bit of money from the bank to make up the difference for the down payment. However I borrowed it on the basis of the business— and the business will pay it out, I hope. That is why I cannot say at this time when I will be taking out some money from the business. It is still comparatively new and it has been a tremendous struggle all the way. I assure you that just as soon as I am able to I will try to lessen your financial burden. You have been very fair about it and I appreciate it deeply.

Having a house of our own is very important to us now. I feel the saving on taxes justifies the purchase. Until I pay up the bank loan it's going to be touch and go—after that, the pressure should ease a little.

Perhaps I seem to be biting off more than I can chew, but if I work hard enough at least I'll have something *to show for it, a permanent home for the children that will someday be theirs. It's little enough inheritance to leave them.*

If there are any further details you would like to have please let me know.

Take care of yourself and believe always that I wish nothing but the best for you.

As Ever—

Lee

37

Thank You, I Think

WHEN R. AND I DIVORCED, WE MADE A PLEDGE to shield the kids from the crap in our relationship. We promised to only speak well of each other and to encourage the relationships our kids had with each of us. And this is the advice/warning I offer to clients going through the same thing. It's the standard, definitive warning to divorcing spouses. Don't bad-mouth the other parent. Your kids need relationships with each parent uncorrupted by your own anger or pain. They need to come to their own independent sense of each parent. You need to love your child more than you hate you ex. Yet sometimes I hear friends freely talking to their grown children about their ex-spouses with disdain, *what an asshole he is, what a fucking loser, I hate that bitch.* It might be true but is it the right thing to do?

Even as a full-grown adult I was carrying a fantasy version of the father who'd abandoned us. I see how I needed that, how it helped me in some twisted way. I see that my mother enabled my fairy tale. She did not want to corrupt my "shiny and untarnished image" of him. But, jeez, I also see how fucked up that is, her letting me walk around with such delusion.

Maybe it's better to just tell the whole damn truth to your kids, your side of what has always got to be a complex story. Or maybe the fantasy relationship I had with my father gave me some of what I needed to build myself a life. Who the fuck knows.

38

The Cruise to War-Torn Lands (2001)

GREEDY, GREEDY, GREEDY. VERY DUMB AND VERY greedy. All these years on the planet and you'd think a person would know better.

The last of my stepfathers had died and my mother says, "I want to take you all on a trip." She says, "It will be *amazing*, the trip of a lifetime." She says, "Anywhere. Pick anywhere you want to go. No expense spared. It's all on me." I imagine there are families where an offer like this does not automatically lead to high anxiety. We were beyond nervous, my sister and I. We'd learned to avoid the less extravagant hooks with strategies like making a suggestion to donate to the Red Cross instead of a birthday gift.

Or at restaurants: *Oh, too late! I gave the waiter my credit card already so the bill is taken care of but thanks so much for offering, mom.* It took over four decades to get that far but at least we got partway there. The traps, though, they just kept getting more alluring and less easy to step over; the calculus more vague and perplexing.

I mean, someone offers you a trip to anywhere in the world, all expenses paid? Come on.

In spite of the dazzle, my sister and I, we're on guard. We remind each other of all the other times. We get palpitations from the memories and laugh about our stupidity. We make pacts and resolutions. We can't be dumb enough to step in that quicksand.

Then my mother says, "Before I die."

Okay, so fine. We're going on a Mediterranean cruise. We figure it will be much easier to tend to her this way, on a ship—no packing and unpacking, no city prowling or country hikes, no high-level negotiations on where to eat three times a day, every single bloody day. We tell her the plan and she says, "That's fine," the way people say 'that's fine' when it's so totally *not* fine. And then she says, "I didn't know they were so expensive. Yeesh!"

Even so, a lot of greed and a little guilt fuck with my judgment and I decide it will be worth whatever it costs to see Croatia on someone else's dime.

* * *

Our cruise leaves from Venice. A whole day to fill in Venice. You wouldn't think that was such a huge challenge, thinking up something to do in that remarkable city. But you'd have to know my mother. *You're walking too fast, my legs hurt, I'm tired, I've already seen that, I'm not interested.* So a gondola ride, what else! It's a beautiful day, we'll be sitting down the whole time, no decisions to make. There are two men there to help my mother get in the gondola, you'd think that would be sufficient. But no. Somehow—and if she were consciously trying, I'm not sure how she could have planned it any better—she falls, half in gondola, half in canal. So, back to the hotel to pass the time until the ship leaves because we can't leave her untended in a foreign city because she doesn't speak Italian and she doesn't know anyone and she might need some help and she's old and she paid for this trip. Way to kick things off!

On the ship morning one: We knock on her cabin door so we can walk her to the dining room for breakfast. She's not coming. She doesn't feel well and we should just go ahead without her.

Mid-day one: She meets us for lunch but is not speaking. We ask if she is okay and she says, "I'm fine." Those two words and that's it for the afternoon, no matter what we ask, no matter how we try.

Evening one: She's not up to anything, will skip dinner and the show, and we should just go on without her, go ahead and have fun why don't you, never mind about me, I'll just stay in my cabin.

Morning two: Ditto.

Mid-day two: Ditto.

Evening two: Ditto.

I am aware this sounds like exaggeration. It is not.

Morning three: My sister says we should try again. Me, I wouldn't have gone yesterday. Then again, my sister is the one who drove into San Francisco on some bogus emergency after she'd already fallen for that once before, also something I wouldn't have done. We have a basket of examples like that, countless times where my sister extended herself far beyond where I was willing to go. I can never settle on who comes out looking worse in that, my sister or me.

So morning three, we again start down one of the windowless corridors that thread the ship, passing door after door after sealed-shut door. Dim, clangy halls where the only sign of life is the predictable crackle that precedes announcements on the PA which, by the way, cannot be escaped. There is not a bathroom, a cocktail lounge, a casino, or a broom closet where you can't hear someone with unrelenting good cheer remind you of shuffleboard on the Lido Deck at 11, The Newlywed Game during cocktail time around the pool on C deck, and Vin the Ventriloquist in the Starlight Room at 10, it's a blue show parents, so tuck those kids in bed and come have some adult time. At least in the corridors it's a respite from the photographers who lurk around every corner, ready to capture a moment. Like I would want a memento of this. Like I could ever forget.

In my real life, I would have the capacity to actually enjoy this, though mostly in an ironic way, I have to cop to that. But if I were here with friends, hey, I'd totally love to take a roll of quarters to the slots or play ping-pong or lie in a deck chair wrapped in a blanket and watch the black night sky with all those stars. But all my natural flippancy and sass and gameness have been drained away and I am running on fumes.

We arrive at her cabin and give a tentative knock. Probably by some amazing intuitive calculation, my mother blithely opens her door, dressed and ready to go. She barely cracks five feet but somehow she looks strangely taller. Her subliminal skills are fierce. She is awesome, how she can take it right to the brink of my very last nerve and then retreat. "I'm starving, " she says. "I'm getting pancakes. And bacon, lots of bacon." She's downright cheery at the breakfast table. "We should make reservations for the show tonight and maybe throw a towel over those beach chairs by the pool, you know, under the awning. How about that couple from Tulsa? You know, the woman with all the red hair, to me it's orange actually, and her husband, I guess it's her husband, with those rings? Did you get a load of them?"

Yes, it's a relief. It's better than yesterday. She's kind of like a real person and I can actually feel my face begin to move into something like an expression. The shards of hope are lodged so deeply inside me, fused into the fabric of my body, permanently embedded. Each time she is a normal person for a minute, the tight grip I have on my guard releases a bit. I'm back in the room, in my body, back to hearing the clatter of trays and silverware, the mid-level chatter of hundreds of breakfasting strangers, my sister and her husband both with something that look like actual smiles on their faces. I am reassured. I am just a little consoled. I am hoodwinked. She stabs into her last bite of pancakes, turns to me, and says, "You know, your sister and I have always been the best-dressed in this family."

Next day: We all head to our respective cabins to escape from the ever-present loudspeaker, get a little rest, and decompress. I actually think that what we are all doing from the moment we get up each day is count the minutes until we can justify announcing that it's afternoon nap time. We all crave the chance to close our cabin doors behind us, my mother included, I am sure. All this forced togetherness. We never spend this much time together. On purpose. So afternoon naps are saving us each from some potential grim, drastic act caused by all of it being just too damn much. So when I hear the commotion outside my sister's cabin during nap time, I know something's up. Without opening my door all I can make out is raised voices too muffled to understand. After a few minutes there's a knock on my door. My sister. Our mother had banged angrily on their door, pushed her way into their cabin, and accused my sister of stealing from her. Like going into her room when she wasn't there, rifling through her purse and suitcase and dresser drawers, and absconding with the loot. It's a ridiculous accusation, out of nowhere, based on nothing, completely unwarranted and founded on exactly zero. So my mother left in a righteous huff and my sister was left feeling, well, everything!

Someone should study her brain. They really should.

This is all totally predictable, of course. Every bit of it. In fact, it would be a minor miracle if she did *not* behave this way since past behavior is the best predictor of future behavior. I learned that in graduate school. So, it's all payment in the pound-of-flesh price tag for this so-called free trip.

I consider faking appendicitis. Or paying however many millions of dollars it would cost to airlift myself the fuck off this fucking ship. I consider jumping into the crazy blue water off Sardinia. I have dinner in my cabin and open my laptop.

Google search: Death on cruise ships.

Preliminary results:

Grant Medeiros—14 from Canada, argues with his parents and jumps overboard while the ship is 12 miles offshore.

Micki Kanesaki—52, was sailing with her lawyer ex-husband when she disappeared in the middle of the night. Her body was later found floating in the sea. She had been murdered by strangulation.

Przemyslaw Moranski—Found hanging by his belt in his cabin, the second travel photographer to die aboard Carnival Inspiration within a few-month period.

Karen Roston—26, on her honeymoon after marrying chiropractor and author Dr. Scott Robin Roston, 36, she was murdered and tossed overboard from Sundance Cruises' Stardancer. Her body found, her husband was convicted of her murder.

Kenneth Gemmell—30, was said to have deliberately plunged 100ft from the balcony of his 11th-floor cabin when the ship, Allure of the Seas, was close to the Mexican coast.

<u>Yang Wenjuan</u>—43, a teacher from mainland China, died when her husband tossed her overboard. He said he found her dead and thoughtfully buried her at sea.

The next day we reach our first port and even though my sister and her husband and I want to take the cable car in Dubrovnik, my mother wants to take the bus tour so we book the bus tour, a small concession because, of course, who's paying for this whole goddamn thing. It's time to meet the launch and we are right back to morning one and the silent treatment. After knocking and pounding and nearly screaming at her door with no response, we find a phone and call. Nada. We enlist the help of a steward and page her. Nothing. Now we're worried because it's true, she *is* old so we convince them to let us into her cabin where she's lying in her bed, in the semi-dark, but not so dark that we can't see that she's awake with an issue of *People* magazine open on her chest. She doesn't want to leave the ship but she'll be fine, we should go have a good time and meet up later for dinner where you can be 1000% sure she will extract her pound of flesh for the sin of leaving her all alone while we blithely and heartlessly go out and have fun on her dime. My fallback position is always this: if you're an adult, you're responsible for your own actions and decisions and I'm not going to waste too much energy trying to figure out what the fugazi you might really mean, just say it, for Christ's sake, mom!

* * *

It's not fun to admit but I can see why my sister has sometimes pegged me as the cold, heartless one. She has been the more charitable of the two of us. Sister, you deserve righteous props. You *are* the more charitable—and maybe the more enmeshed, that could be it, too. And she has her husband with her on this nightmare so they can close the cabin door behind them and do whatever it is they do to help her re-inflate her battered psyche. I close my door and that empty room only concentrates my rage and my confusion and my despair. In that room there is not a witness to testify, no caregiver to comfort, and no one even to certify my sanity. At the same time, this small cabin is my only refuge on what is now the giant floating prison that I walked into willingly, locking the door behind me.

Those ten days will live on as contenders for the worst ten days of my life and, believe me, I have had my share of worst days independent of my mother's shenanigans. By the time the ship docked and we boarded the plane and traveled the interminably long flight back to the West Coast where I could finally, finally, finally turn the lock in my door and walk into the blessed, uncomplicated silence of my home—my private, singular, quiet, solitary home—there was not much left of me. Yes, of course I was not a child soldier in Uganda or a Bulgarian girl sold into prostitution. An annoying mother on a Mediterranean cruise is a problem of the privileged that even I—suffering through it—have limited sympathy for. The best I can say is that it was as though every molecule in my body had been deflated; that wherever it is that our life force resides, that place in me was drained to bone dry. I was flattened and empty; airless; bloodless and gutless and afraid that I would never recover my soul.

39

My Mother Writes Poetry

Just I by Lee E.

I find, with time, that no one can repair my soul
And no one can repay the things I stole.
Not mother, lover, child or friend
Can touch my soul with their hand.
Just I.
When love was given, snatched away
Who paid the piper for his play.
I bounce my thoughts and all for naught.
They all escape, we who are caught.
Just I.
And when the anguish of my soul commands
Who is there to listen and understand.
Just I.

40

My Father Begs for Help From a Man
Whom I Believe is His Brother,
Whom I Guess is My Uncle (1968)

Dear Sy,

I need your help urgently, even desperately, and turn to you as my last resort. I need a loan of $3500, $500 of it before the end of the month and the rest as soon after as possible. I'll repay it in full in not less than 18 months, almost certainly within a year, possibly sooner. I'm willing to pay almost any rate of interest. If you have to borrow it, for example, I can pay half again as much interest as it costs you.

As you may have guessed, things have been going to hell with me since my former marriage started going sour, which is why I've withdrawn into this shell and cut myself offfrom you and everyone else. My ex-wife's sadistic treatment pulled me so far down mentally and emotionally that my work got steadily worse, until around the middle of 1959 I lost my job at the 4-A's. Through a stroke of luck the BVI job came looking for me 6 or 7 months later. But things kept going downhill at home, around the end of 1960 I had had all I could stomach and accepted the invitation she had been throwing at me for years to get the hell out, and the divorce became official a few years later. Through all this, my ex-wife treated me to such savage harassment with lawyers, nppocess-servers, lies, slanders behind my back, and financial pressures, that it got to be almost more than I could do just to get through one day, and one night, at a time. I think I did a good job for BVI, but I had no emotional reserves to take the constant personality frictions, and I finally blew up on them and got canned there, too, near the end of 1966. I've been out of work ever since, over a year and a half.

There may be a job for me at the advertising agency I used while at BVI, or at least they suggested I come talk with them. But in my depressed state I have no confidence that I can cope with the personal wear and tear that goes with any job in an advertising agency. Instead I've been trying to make a business of my own, in which I can earn some kind of living without having to be constantly answerable to other people.

What I'm working on is a service for dentists, to help improve their human relations and communication with patients. This is the biggest need in dentistry today, most dentists recognize the need, a lot of them are doing something about it, and my material is better than anything else available. My basic ideas came out of the work at BVI, but I've improved them considerably. I've been testing the service with a small group of dentists here in Scarsdale who with whom I've been meeting two or three days a month since last fall, and it works. They've put me in touch with a large, important and influential group in Nassau County. The Nassau leaders like what I have to offer, and I'm negotiating with them for some kind of group arrangement for their membership, which would get me off the ground with a contract of ten to twenty thousand dollars.

The only trouble is that they all move so slowly, and that no income would be available until some time in the fall, and I can't last that long. Without your help I won't be able to pay my rent Jyly 1. Last December I had what I thought was a firm commitment for a loan of $5000 if I needed it, but for reasons too complicated to explain that fell through when I went to collect on it. When that happened I began looking for some kind of temporary or part time work to tide me over, but so far haven't even come close; this is still a possibility, but is certainly going to take more time than I have left. Unless you can help me, it looks like I'm dead. I am so low and dispirited, and so sick of the whole fucking mess, that if it comes to the point where I can't pay the rent, and they come to throw me out, I don't think there's going to be much choice but to finish myself off with the sleeping tablets.

Forgive me for unloading my troubles on you. I just hope to God things have been better with you than they have with me. Please help me. I have nowhere else left to turn.

41

Lilacs (2005)

WHEN I WAS A CHILD I BELIEVED THAT WHEN you die, at that very moment of your death, you are somehow infused with every single answer to every single question. Like some non-verbal osmosis the answers would all be there: where does the sky end, is there a God, why are we here, do aliens exist, what really happened to my dog, Joey, anyway? Silently, instantly you would know. Maybe this is a typical childhood vision of death, one that mitigates the terror. Or maybe it's the through narrative of my own singular life, how profound and essential the need to fill in all the blank spaces and get some answers for once.

I only remembered that childhood construction of death as I scraped my chair across the linoleum floor to the bedside of my dying mother, probably knocked back into my conscious awareness by that staggeringly unexpected and fuckingly uncharacteristic statement of hers—*If you have any questions, now's the time to ask.* Jesus, woman! You've got to be fucking kidding.

The other thing I realized in that moment was that what she was offering was the one and only thing I wanted from her. Sure, as a child I wanted other things. I wanted toys, I wanted a pony, I wanted straight hair, I wanted freely given gifts, I wanted two parents. But as an adult what I have craved is answers.

So I take her hand and, though she closes her eyes, I lean closer to her face while some silent, frantic calculator inside me starts to spin. I don't have a list prepared because who could have predicted this opportunity. I can't pull a yellowed square of paper from my wallet, tearing at the folds from all those years of carrying it around. Do I start with the most important questions or work up to them? And what the fuck are the most important questions anyway? How much time do I have, how many questions am I allowed? Can I actually keep myself from shaking her or slapping her half-dead face, or sobbing so hard that not even the first question can make it to the surface?

Take a breath, Liz. It would be wrong to start with who are we? Or why are you like this? Or, what the hell? Start with something not at all threatening and work up to the big stuff. Start with something small, something concrete. Something you can hold onto and keep, maybe tucked in a locket around your neck.

"Where did you live when you first came here, to this country, when you came here as a child? What kind of place was it?"

My mother closes her eyes. I do that too when I am thinking hard or trying to remember something just out of reach. And you know how you can practically see the thinking that's going on behind closed eyes sometimes? How the churning mental wheels can somehow show behind closed eyes? That's *not* how she looks. She closes her eyes and takes a nap.

Seriously.

Give it a minute.

"Mom!" I say, "Are you awake?"

Give it a minute.

"I'm awake," she says. "I'm just resting."

She opens her eyes and again I ask, "Where did you live, when you were a kid? What kind of place was it when you first came here? Was it a house? An apartment?"

And again she closes her eyes.

So here's this woman, on her deathbed, her actual deathbed, and she's opened the door and she's told me to ask and I have and now she needs to rest. Yes, of course, she needs to rest. If you're dying, you need to rest but after four or five more rounds of me asking and her "napping," after a while I turn on the

TV because it's just better to watch *The Price Is Right*. Well, fuck me for not knowing better, anyway. And fuck me for not leaving her alone and letting her be herself at the end without holding up a mirror to her insanity.

"Lilacs," she says.

"Excuse me?" I say, because I'm not even sure she said anything, maybe it was the TV or somebody out in the hall.

"Lilacs," she says. "I remember lilacs."

And that was it. I tried, believe me, I tried. In every legal way I knew how. She lived for two more days and was conscious for much of that time but that was what she was willing to give me. Lilacs.

42

Dear Mom (2005)

Dear Mom:

I am so sorry.

You told me you weren't feeling well. Of course, you always said that, that you weren't feeling well. We heard that all the time.

But still.

You said you had some kind of bump thing on your stomach but this time it's a bump, last time it was a sharp pain, before that a strange sensation in your head, three years ago you had a toothache the dentist wouldn't or couldn't help you with, and before that

*your psychiatrist didn't care that you were depressed
and on and on. In fact, I don't remember a time when
you didn't have a bump or a pain or a weird feeling or
a disinterested doctor or a dizzy spell.*

But still.

*You told me it was a pretty big bump, a soft lumpish
thing as big as your fist. I said what I always said,
you'd better go see your doctor. He said what we all
said, what we all believed. It's nothing. It's a benign
sebaceous cyst, just some fluid-filled thing that will
go away on its own but go ahead and use a warm
compress, couldn't hurt.*

Two weeks later you were dead.

*Afterwards they determined it was lung cancer
but only after following the scavenger hunt of clues
that eventually led them back to the original source.
They started at the bump—not a sebaceous cyst but a
malignant tumor, big as your fist, big enough that you
could see it through your clothes from across the room.
The next clue was hidden in your liver so I guess that
explains the pain in your side, huh. From the liver
to the bones, the muscle cramps in your left leg you
complained about over and over and over again and
finally to the lung cancer that had metastasized into
every organ in your body.*

I am so sorry.

But still.

*I mean, what did you expect? Your other daughter
left work, found someone to watch her infant daughter,*

drove the choked Bay Bridge into San Francisco in rush hour traffic only to find that no, actually you were fine, you didn't mean to scare her when you said you'd just called 911, you hadn't actually done that, she'd misunderstood. Or the time you called her at 3 A.M., you sobbing so hard she had no way of knowing what you were saying, trying to figure out what was wrong and finally getting in her car and again crossing the Bay Bridge into the black San Francisco night to find you fast asleep. Or the time on the first day of one of my visits that you told me you had been gushing blood every time you went to the bathroom—your word, gushing—and I called your doctor who told me to take you right to the ER where, after sitting in the straight-backed chairs for two hours, when it was finally our turn, you told the doctor that no, not really, you actually hadn't been bleeding, you didn't really know why you were there but you came because I wanted you to. This is how it went.

But still.

This time. This one time. And what we did was roll our eyes and slam down the phone and swear and commiserate and hate you all over again.

I am so sorry.

Even still.

Love,

Liz

43

Three Examples of
My Father's Communications
(1970, 1994, & 1996)

November 4, 1970

Mr. Jerome Heller
Garth Manor Corp
80 Lefferts Avenue
Brooklyn, N. Y.

Dear Mr. Heller:

Monday afternoon, day before yesterday, I found stuck behind the door-knob the eviction notice for next Monday the 9th.

This is the first I've heard about the judgment which led to it. It leaves me no time to dispose adequately of my furnishings, or to make arrangements for a place to go, or to pursue my efforts to raise money, or to find a job to tide me over.

As I think I've hinted, the last few months have been a nightmare for me with a succession of severe personal and emotional problems that have brought me to a state of very deep depression. A couple of times it has brought me close to doing away with myself—something I can mention now because I'm coming out of it and any such danger is past.

I freely acknowledge my obligation to you, and my intention to repay it in full, with interest, as soon as I'm able. But that depends on a reasonable chance to rehabilitate myself.

May I make this suggestion? Let me have until the end of the month. If I can't come up with the back rent by then, I'll move out voluntarily and you won't have to go to the expense of evicting me. And as quickly as I'm able, I'll pay up what I owe you.

In effect, you'd be gambling three weeks rental income to make it possible for me to pay the $1,000 arrears, plus saving you the cost of eviction.

Sincerely,

cc: Mr. Gilbert Balter
bcc: Mr. Alexander K Perlman, Legal Aid

22 August 1994

Telephone Preference Service
Direct Marketing Association
PO Box 9014
Farmingdale NY 11735-9014

Gentlemen:

I have two telephone lines:

> 610-666-1150
> 610-666-5702

When I answer one of those arrogant, intrusive, inconsiderate telemarketing calls, I tell the caller I'll speak with him/her only after he/she gives me his/her name and home number.

They never do, of course. Meaning it's OK for *them* to bother the hell out of *me*—not for *me* to bother the hell out of *them*.

It's *not* OK for them to bother the hell out of me. You jerks have *always* been the biggest single public pain in the ass. With this telepersecution plague you've gone totally over the edge. The whole putrid lot of you ought to have *your* asses kicked—into the sewers where you belong.

Now, God damn you, *take my name off every one of your lists.*

Repeat: *take my name off every one of your lists.*

I hope your whole stinking, scrofulous crew rots in hell. And I mean that

Very, very sincerely,

March 15, 1996

RiteAid Pharmacy
1119 Pawlings Rd.
Audubon, PA 19403

Dear Store Manager:

WHY AUDUBON RITEAID IS NO LONGER MY DRUG STORE

1. The store needs vacuuming. I understand this is a temporary location, but the store is depressingly grungy.

2. About one Rx in four was filled with a child proof cap, despite my checking "no child-proof cap" **each time** I picked up an Rx. The child proof caps used must be the cheapest available, because they are almost impossible to open.

3. Pharmacist HLK is excellent, and the older woman at the cash register at the front is courteous, competent and friendly. The rest of the staff was noticeably unfriendly or busy chatting during my many visits. I was never given any drug information beyond the printed slip of paper, except by HLK.

4. The price label on the Cola Syrup for nausea obscured the directions for use of the product. The person on duty did read me labeling from another bottle when I called.

5. The large sign advertising cigarettes on the window is out of place in a store selling products to promote better health, and cure illness.

Your arrival in the Audubon Shopping Center is a loss for the community.

Sincerely,

44

August's Visit, Part One (1978)

OVER THE YEARS I'VE WORKED WITH CLIENTS who are dealing with the aftermath of emotional shock. It could be the result of a car crash, a sudden death, or any other frightening event. It could be an emotionally traumatic childhood experience. There's no DSM V diagnosis for emotional shock and the symptoms can be wide and varied. I've seen people who are increasingly anxious and others who are depressed and withdrawn. Some shut down emotionally, others are overly sensitive. Just depends. But emotional shock is damage to the psyche, no matter how it is expressed. Sometimes symptoms resolve quickly. Other times they endure.

* * *

It had been weeks, or I don't know, maybe it was months, since I sat around my father's chipped linoleum table with him and his girlfriend, Martha. Sure, by that time my feet were on the ground. Yes, I was making lunches for my kids. And, though it was perhaps not the best idea, I was working as a freshly-minted therapist. (Those poor clients. I should search them out and refund them their money. Not that any new therapist is so great but me, I really was no good at that time. How could someone holding so tightly to a chimera, trying so hard to resist the truth, how could she possibly be of any help to another soul in the journey of self-discovery? I mean, seriously.)

But when the phone rang and there he was on the other end, I was still gripping tight to the picture I'd held of him since I was a little girl. My father. My soulmate. My genius. My faraway prince. My strong, dark energy. My normal. I was still holding but my knuckles were mighty white.

He called me to say that he and Martha were taking a road trip to somewhere in, I think, Minnesota or Michigan or Iowa or somewhere beyond where I lived to visit one of her kids. Cleveland was on the way and maybe they could stop at my place for the night and it would be so nice to meet his grandchildren, anyway. And, oh, he says, before he hangs up, don't tell Martha, you know, about the Jewish thing.

She doesn't know and I want to keep it that way. Had we even mentioned the "Jewish thing?" I don't think we had but I say, yes, come to Cleveland, stay in my house, meet your grandchildren and no, I won't tell.

We sit in my living room—my father, his girlfriend, my husband, and I. My two small girls running in and out, ready for bed in their matching Winnie-the-Pooh footies. He's not shy, launches right in and doesn't stop talking, doesn't look over, when the girls tug at my sleeve wanting juice or something off the plate on the coffee table. He's working on some article for a science journal, Martha is a chemist, he reminds me. Tennis, he still loves tennis, he says, and I'm waving the girls into the kitchen while I'm nodding and listening and agreeing. He is enthralled with Brahms these days. Did I understand the complexity and profundity, the man was a genius. I did—I think I did—understand, and I agree yes, a genius but no, I haven't learned the Rhapsody in B minor, that's way above me, I think I have the music somewhere, I don't know where, but no, I really don't think I can play it and no, I have no idea why more symphony orchestras don't put Brahms on the program, and then it's about some writer I've never heard of who also doesn't get enough acclaim, I really should write down these titles, can I get some paper and a pen and now the words dissolve into letters and the letters are just sounds and I am back at their linoleum table and it's tennis and the Panama Canal and Elvis fucking Presley and talking and talking and talking and my face is burning hot and blood beats behind my eyes.

"Stop," I say. "I can't do this."

45

The Academy Award for Best Actress (2005)

Someone I know won an Oscar and every year after was allowed to bring one guest to the Academy Awards. One year I was that guest. Anyone who knows me understands. The fucking Academy Awards! I shopped for the perfect dress. I reserved a room just across the street from the venue about a year ahead of time. I lost weight. I got my hair cut. I imagined I was a star and wrote an acceptance speech.

The day arrives and about an hour before the pre-show red carpet doings I start to prep. A long, relaxing bath spiked with lavender oil. More time than I have ever taken on my hair and make-up, more than even on my wedding day(s). Slip into the long, fire engine red dress with the slit up the front of the right leg. Strappy sandals and chandelier earrings. Ten minutes to relax and I'm ready for my close-up, Mr. DeMille. One foot is right over the threshold and the phone rings. My mother is in the hospital. The nurse says things don't look good. She says your mother is in severe pain, the worst of her life, she says, and we're waiting for the test results but your mother doesn't look good. She is moaning and incoherent. She keeps saying she wants you to come. She says you should get here as soon as you can. And of course I will go because what if she dies and I don't see her and she knows I chose the Oscars over her and I can't hold her hand and she goes to her death ruined by her failures as a parent and neither one of us ever feels the solace of absolution.

In the space of ten minutes I have taken off my red dress, thrown it into my suitcase with the rest of my crap, called the airline, checked out of the hotel, summoned a taxi, and driver, step on it, I'm going to LAX.

The television is on in my mother's room and when I walk in, breathless from hustling down the hall, I can hear Jon Stewart winding up his opening shtick. My mother is sitting up in bed, sipping on a cranberry juice, wearing a T-shirt that says Gucci in gold, very definitely alive. Her hair, ravaged by decades of perms and dye-jobs from platinum to raven black, now looking strangely like orange cotton candy. She is tickled pink to see me. "Lizzie," she says, waving her hand wildly at the TV. "I saw you in the crowd, in the red carpet thing, I told the nurse, that's my daughter!"

Yeah, well, here's the thing. You did *not* just see me in the red carpet thing because it was happening exactly while I was harping at the cab driver to go faster, faster because I had to rush to make the goddamn flight so I could harp at another cab driver to go faster, faster so I could run out of breath down the long hospital corridor and make it to the bedside of my dying mother. You do not get to rip me away from the Oscars *and* get bragging rights about look that's *my* daughter on the red carpet too. You have to choose, woman! You don't get to pull one of your famous double binds on me, not today, not now, not again, no!

The flight home is a hot mess nightmare. I'm standby so what I get is just about the last row, middle seat. It's a pouring down monster storm, lightning and thunder cut the night sky, the plane lurching so much that several people grab their vomit bags, a couple too late. The man next to me clamps my arm, this close to drawing blood. I'm scared too, of course, but my fear seems somehow blunted, probably pushed to the side by the sack of other feelings I'm hauling home. I just don't have room for the panic I would normally be feeling. Mostly I'm numb. When we finally land, the plane erupts in the applause of relief. Outside, I can barely muster the energy to lift my arm to hail a cab in what continues to be a deluge. On the way home the cab hydroplanes across the Fremont Bridge. Again, under usual circumstances this would be a fist-clenching, rapid-heart-beating, foot-jamming-into-pretend-brakes-in-the-backseat kind of experience that would send me almost over the edge to a full-blown panic attack but, instead, I'm kind of complacent, weirdly relaxed, or maybe just too empty to give a shit. Visibility is about zero and lightning flashes perilously close to the bridge, at least that's what it looks like, and when the cabby finally pulls up in front of my building, I'm not even sure if I have what it takes to open the door. Maybe I'll just live in the back seat of the cab. But I make it out, lug my suitcase packed with that red hot slinky dress with the slit up the right thigh into the building, ride the elevator up to my floor, turn the key, and I'm in. I'm home again and I have not been to the Academy Awards, I have not worn my red dress, my mother is still alive, and I have had nothing to eat since breakfast. But I am home, in my own space. My sanctuary. Mostly I just want to fall into bed but I grab a carrot, turn off the kitchen lights, and…

Anyone who's ever aspirated something like a taco chip (I have), or a piece of chicken (I have), or a chunk of apple (yep), knows how terrifying those moments can be. It's its own special kind of horror. So, again, if I were my normal self, I would be panicked, begging the atheists' god, flinging wildly against every hard object in sight in an attempt to Heimlich myself, desperately *not* ready to die. Instead what I feel is irony. That's the only word. It's all just too fucking ironic. After all that and this is how it ends? Perfect. Just perfect.

46

One Thing I'm Good At

SELF-SOOTHING

47

Some Relative of Mine, But Who?
(1932)

LAST TRIBUTE PAID RABBI ISAAC BICK

More than 1000 Persons Attend Funeral Services
at Sons of Jacob Synagogue

Son Loses His Race

Stormy Weather Forces Him to Abandon Airplane Flight
for Train at Chicago

Funeral services for Rabbi Isaac Bick, of Sons of Jacob Congregation Synagogue, Douglas Avenue, were held yesterday afternoon in the presence of nearly a score of rabbis and more than 1000 members of the laity, but while a son of the rabbi was still hurrying to this city from St. Louis by train and airplane.

Rabbi Bick died Tuesday morning of a heart attack. He was 63 years old. In order to allow the son, Rabbi Herman Bick of St. Louis, to reach Providence in time for the services, an exception to Jewish religious law was allowed and the funeral was postponed until yesterday noon.

The son took a plane in St. Louis, intending to fly here, but stormy weather conditions forced him to land in Chicago and proceed from there by train. He was expected to arrive in Providence at 5 o'clock yesterday afternoon, several hours after the burial. It was explained that no further postponement could be made because under Jewish law burial must take place before sundown. Another son, a rabbi in New York, was present.

Probably the largest aggregation of rabbis witnessed here on one occasion gathered for the funeral. Most local rabbis attended and there were rabbis from New York, Boston, Fall River, New Bedford and Chelsea, Mass.

Hundreds lined the street in front of the Bick home at 157 Orms street, from where the casket was carried on the shoulders of eight rabbis to the synagogue on Douglas Avenue. The synagogue was crowded to capacity, with more than 500 persons in the main hall and an almost equal number of women in the gallery. Women are barred from the main floor of orthodox synagogues and sit in the gallery during services.

Max Richter, president of the Sons of Jacob Congregation, presided at the services in the synagogue, and eulogies were delivered by several rabbis. There was audible weeping in the gallery as the speakers extolled the virtues of Rabbi Bick as a teacher and spiritual guide. Burial was in Lincoln Park Cemetery.

Among the rabbis who attended were David Bachrach, O.W. Werner and Joshua Werner, all of this city; Chaim Bick, Moses Bick and Shoel Bick, all of New York; H. Perlov of Brooklyn, N. Twersky of Chelsea, Abraham Lipschitz of Fall River and Rabbi A. Popkin of New Bedford. Israel E. Freidman represented the Yeshiva College of New York.

A squad of five patrolmen from the Precinct 2 station under Sergt. R.A. Campbell directed traffic in front of the house and the synagogue. The funeral procession was escorted by motorcycle men to the city limits.

48

Letter from My Father's Wife (1996)

11/18/96

Dear Liz:

Yesterday I began 5am to go through the Gus things in the attic and in the back of my file cabinets, and it took a long time.

I had looked at some of the stuff briefly over the years, but never went through it carefully, because it wasn't mine, and I didn't really feel that interested.

All the checks, bank statements and tax returns from 1960 to the present were there. I saved the tax returns and a small sample of the rest of the financial stuff. There are letters written during the 1960's, fewer than 20 in all, between Gus and your mother. (He saved carbons.)

The thing that particularly made me write this though, are the letters you wrote to your father begging to see him. I can never explain or excuse what he did.

I have his application for social security, giving his parents names, his place of birth, etc. I also have your parent's divorce decree, which was needed when he married me in 1982. By the way, your mother could collect a Social Security widow's benefit of about $1100/month if she wishes, depending on whether that is more than her own benefit. (I just learned this last Thursday.)

I know that Gus is always an issue in your life; each stage ...

I know that Gus is always an issue in your life, each stage of life brings a re-examination of core relationships.

Please let me know if you have an interest in this material.

Best wishes,

Martha

49

What My Mother Taught Me

- Entertaining is fun. Keep the cupboard stocked so you can throw together a spur-of-the-moment dinner party or cocktail gathering—pouches of homemade pasta sauce in the freezer, cheese and crackers, jars of cornichons, and tins of pâté and smoked oysters. Don't be afraid to try new recipes. What's the worst that could happen? The more the merrier, so just squeeze them around the table.

- Meet as many important people as you can and work hard to make them your friends.

- Be cultured and sophisticated—that means art, music, theater, literature.

- Always try to sound like you know more than you do and that you're the one in the room with the most information. Make it look like you know something about everything, except it's okay to be dumb about sports; in fact it's kind of cute.

- Creative people are the best people.

- Seduction is your currency.

- Don't worry too much about propriety. Be outrageous and unconventional. Swear, ask personal questions, reveal personal-like information but keep your deepest self hidden from view.

- Be surprisingly shrewd.

- Overestimate your looks, talents, and intelligence.

- Maintain a slippery moral compass.

- Be sassy and bold and unconcerned about convention.

- Treat the man in your life coldly and with disdain. Throw yourself on your sword and apologize with tears when he gets fed up. Reel him back in and start all over with contempt.

- Be game.

- It's not enough to be a housewife.

- Throw in foreign words and phrases any time you get a chance. Le français est le meilleur; Latin is second best.

- Be a character.

- You can't rely on anyone so take care of your own damn self.

- Be youthful and unshockable.

- Be a man's woman.

- You're famous or you're nothing.

- Dance and sing.

- Remember there's a price tag for every gift given and strings attached to every act of kindness.

- Try and get all the attention focused on yourself at all times. If you feel it slipping away, find some way to yank it back.

- Be a good liar. A very good liar.

- Be flirtatious with every man you meet and have sex with anyone who wants to have sex with you; that they want you is the most important thing.

- Develop a bottomless pit of sucking need.

50

Letter from Cousin Murray (1986)

Our Aunt Millie had a son named Murray, who would be our cousin, right? He lives in Israel and now is sadly demented so, once again, no chance for any concrete information. And even if he were *compos mentis* I doubt he'd be the person to turn to for answers. He fancied himself the family historian but this is the extent of what we learned from him:

Dear Margaret,

It was good speaking with you the other day and welcoming you back to our family. Millie asked me to thank you for calling her. She enjoyed immensely speaking with you.

There is so much to say in order to acquaint you with the family you haven't known these many years. Where do I begin? This is a family so rich in history. Many of its members made their mark on history before fading into dust. Imagine a man known as the "seer of Lublin" and another considered to be the wisest, most brilliant man of his age. But I needn't go so far back to find family members who did things beyond the norm or who were involved in situations which defy logic.

Abe was not Lee's and my mother's only brother. There was another. His name was Simcha, named for the great Reb Simcha, our great great grandfather. When young Simcha was only 16, he had already been ordained a rabbi. Our grandfather, no small scholar himself, often consulted him. According to Millie, he had a saintly disposition. Unfortunately, he fell ill. A Christian maid was obtained to care for Simcha, a woman who was not quite all there. However, every Friday night, Sabbath eve, the woman became completely lucid and remained so until sundown Saturday.

One Friday evening, Simcha went to sleep as usual. When he awoke in the morning he told of a strange dream that he had. A very tall man, dressed entirely in black, with full red beard, walked toward him. Simcha mentioned a small detail. The man was twirling a gold keychain about his finger. He approached Simcha in the dream and touched him on the shoulder. When Simcha awakened, that arm was paralyzed. Our grandfather was very shaken when young Simcha mentioned the small detail of the keychain. It was something young Simcha had never been told. This was something Reb Simcha did. Nor were there any photographs of Reb Simcha, yet the young man described him perfectly. The following Friday evening, Simcha again went to sleep. When he awoke in the morning, he told the family that he had again seen the red-bearded man. This time, the man beckoned to him. On hearing this, grandfather burst into tears. Within the week, young Simcha died.

There is another story which Millie, who is considerably older than Lee, can attest to. In the early days of this century, our grandmother and grandfather planned to take a train. They were escorted to the railway station where grandfather purchased two tickets. Then they all went out on the platform to await the train. Presently the train thundered into the station, belching steam and chuddering to a halt. Our grandparents said their goodbyes and turned to board the train. Their path was blocked by a giant in a black conductor's uniform, with stiff brimmed cap. Our grandfather was six feet tall, a veritable giant in his day, yet this smooth shaven trainman was perhaps a head taller and stood squarely in grandfather's way.

"You can't get on this train," the conductor said.

"We have tickets," grandfather said and showed them.

The conductor spread his huge arms, effectively preventing grandfather from walking around him.

Grandfather cast glances to the left and right. Along the length of the train, people were boarding unhindered. Grandfather pleaded, bellowed, tried to reason with the conductor, but it did no good.

Finally, the train began to inch forward, picking up speed as it moved. Still the conductor stood their [sic], repeating the one sentence, "You can't get on this train." The train pulled out of the station and rumbled off toward the horizon. Furious, grandfather reentered the station, leaving the giant conductor standing on the platform, sought out the stationmaster who had sold him, and berated him.

The stationmaster was puzzled. He knew nothing of a giant conductor. With grandfather at his side, the stationmaster went back out to the platform. There was no conductor to be seen. Nor did anyone see this giant leave the town. He was never seen again. And the train? It fell from a bridge, killing everyone aboard. I will put no interpretations on this, or on other things which I will put to paper at another time.

I guess I've become the archivist of the family. No one else appears to be at all that interested. For better or worse, I'm haunted by these characters out of our past. But for them, we wouldn't exist. There are many who would deny the past. They say, "big deal" or "who cares?" I care and, to me, that's all that matters. And so they reach out to me over the centuries. They live because they aren't forgotten. I have three children and none of them is particularly interested in all I've discovered. My sister's two children don't care either. Perhaps ours will be the last generation to carry this torch of history and after us, perhaps it will all be lost. I mourn for this loss, because this past, so long denied to you, enriches us all.

Already memories are fading and many of our relatives have been consigned to graves forgotten for all time. There was Hinde, Lee's and Millie's aunt, plain Hinde, unloved Hinde, who was outshone by Edith, a vivacious blonde who totally overshadowed her sister. A young man came on the scene who loved Hinde, but our great grandfather would have none of that. His family was of more humble origins and he forbade Hinde from seeing the young man and so he left the scene. There was to be no other. Hinde grew older, deafer, more bitter. Finally, delusions developed. People were plotting against her. She died a poor, lonely old wretch and today is all but forgotten. This is probably the first mention made of this unfortune [sic] *in more than 25 years.*

I hope I haven't bored you with my memories and tales. If you prefer, there are other things I can write about, dear cousin. The important thing is that we've met once more.

Love,

Murray

To which I say: Cousin Murray, fucking ridiculous and fucking not helpful.

51

August's Visit, Part Two— Or, the Last Time I Saw My Father (1978)

M Y FATHER'S TRUNCATED VISIT WAS ONLY THE third time I'd seen him since that fateful day at Rockefeller Center when I was around ten or eleven. I didn't know when I opened my home to him that the visit would be so short and that it would be the very last time I had any contact with him. Even though he was supposed to spend the night, I demanded he leave my house. Kicking him out was maybe the bravest act of my life. This is how it went down: After the "How was your drive?" and "Did you find us okay?"

and "Can I get you something to drink?," we sat down on my comfy living room furniture and he launched in and because my anesthesia had not yet worn off completely, I listened. I listened to a detailed synopsis of Freud's *Moses and Monotheism.* I listened to a rant about the misuse of the objective pronoun. I listened to an exhaustive description of the resurfacing of his neighborhood tennis court. I listened and I listened and kept listening until I couldn't let even one more syllable in. And it wasn't just the yammering on about all kinds of intellectual, pretentious bullshit or the trivial nonsense of his life that meant less than nothing to me. Why the fuck do I care that his tennis partner had to fucking have his fucking knee replaced? It wasn't *just* that. It was how he couldn't even bother turning his head to take just a quick glance at those two little girls in their footies and pigtails who couldn't be sweeter or cuter or more re-lated to him. It was keeping his twisted secret. It was sitting at his linoleum table like it was just a normal day. It was lunch with him around the ice rink those many decades ago. It was leaving me to be mothered by her. It was twenty years of missed birthdays and holidays and bruised knees and vacations and recitals and proms and graduations and weddings and broken hearts. It was taking a pickaxe to my illusions. It was my denseness and it was my denial.

So I said, "Stop." I said, "I can't do this" and then I said, "I need you to tell me why."

When he met me at Kennedy Airport and threw his arms around me, he was happy to see me. He really did seem genuinely happy. But in my living room, at that moment when I couldn't bear one more fraudulent word, I just knew that okay, yes, he had been happy to see me but it was the kind of happy you'd be if you ran into someone you went to college with and hadn't seen in twenty years, all hail fellow well met. *How ya been, buddy? Jeez, it's been so long. You look great!* That kind of happy.

And when I said I had some questions, when I asked him why he'd never contacted us, how he could do that to his own children, well, that was the end of happy to see me. Just like that he was dark with bitter outrage. He was affronted and aggrieved. His words were spitting darts and his eyes the blackest black. He turned to face me—was that actually the first time?—and he said he owed no one, not that fucking bitch mother of yours, not you, not your sister, I don't owe anyone any explanation, I'm done with that bullshit.

So was I.

Two weeks later, his wife called me. He loves you, she said. I know he does. I don't know why he's like this, she said, I can't explain it but I have to believe he loves you. He's just not capable, she said, please understand. But my ability to make him into a father who loved me was eroded beyond recovery. Now it was just righteous anger.

Before we hung up I had this wonderful and weirdly comforting sense of irony. He would expect me to understand the concept of a Faustian bargain. He would want to educate me and quiz me on the original source material—Marlowe and Goethe and Gounod. He would be contemptuous of anyone foolish enough to enter into such a weak-hearted deal. Okay, fine. You're right. So I told her about the secret he'd asked me to keep from her. There. Fuck you.

52

Dear Daddy (around 1962)

(after 7/9/62)

Elizabeth Nelson
Weston, Conn.

Dear Daddy,

I was just reading
over some old letters of
mine and I came across
one of yours. I read it about
five times ... over and
over and, oh dad, I can't
help crying.. I must see
you. Please, please, please..
can I come in some evening
soon. There are so many
things I want to talk to you
about and, I don't know
if you realize or notice this
but, you and I were closest
because we were and are the
most alike.

Again, I implore you –
please may I see you –

(over)

Please write me back as soon as possible. Our new address is:

Ridge Road

All my love always,

Liz

P.S. You probably won't believe me but mother doesn't even know I wrote this!

53

What My Father Taught Me

- Develop an intense, abiding, object hunger for men.

54

Genealogy

MY SISTER AND I GREW UP NEVER MEETING A single relative—other than our mother and father, of course. Not a grandmother or grandfather, an aunt or uncle, a cousin or second cousin or third cousin twice-removed. No one. I can't recall ever giving it much thought and, hard to believe, it was just something we all sort of took for granted. It was the way our family was. Even so, looking back at the me in those days, there is a vague feeling, something I'd call empty. Something floaty and unmoored. While my friends saw their annoying cousins every year at Thanksgiving or got five bucks from their Aunt Caroline every birthday or learned to make their grandmother's special banana bread, not us. No cards came in the mail, no cousins to fight with, no recipes handed down.

It was well into my middle age that my sister made contact with Millie—one of my mother's eight (!) siblings as it turns out—and then with Millie's son Murray, our cousin. And it was through Murray we learned that, like every other human on earth, we did have relatives after all, though what he wanted us to hear was a collection of apocryphal, bullshit folklore. Still, by some circuitous route we came across a fat, two-volume book called *The Unbroken Chain*, and look at that, it seems we do have relatives!

- Elizabeth and Margaret Nelson (my sister and I).

- Lee Bick (married to August Nelson née Horowitz) MY MOTHER (one of eight children!).

- Rabbi Saul Issachar Bick (1883–April 1971) GRANDFATHER.

- Rabbi Isaac Bick (1865–December 6, 1932) GREAT-GRANDFATHER.

- R. Simcha Bick (1829–1896) GREAT-GREAT-GRANDFATHER.

- Pesia Rappoport (wife of R. Saul Issachar Berish Bick).

- R. Zvi Arieh Rappoport, A.B.D. Medzibezh (d. 1803). See note 1.

- Miriam Emden (married to R. Dov Berish Rappoport, A.B.D. Medzibezh).

- R. Meir Emden, A.B.D. Constantin, born 1717.

- R. Jacob Israel Emden (June 4, 1697–April 19, 1776). See note 2.

- R. Zvi Hirsch Ashkenazi (1660–1718).

- R. Jacob Ashkenazi Zak (d. 1697).

- Daughter of R. Jacob Heschel [name unknown] (married to R. Benjamin Zeev Zak, rabbi in Lublin).

- R. Jacob Heschel (also known as Rabbi Jacob of Lublin).

- Daughter of R. Jacob Halevi [name unknown] (married to R. Ephraim Naftali Hirsch, A.B.D. Ludmir).

- Bonah Katzenellenbogen (wife of R. Jacob Halevi).

- R. Meir Katzenellenbogen, the Maharam of Padua (1482–1564). See note 3.

- Daughter of R. Jehiel Luria [name unknown] (married to R. Isaac Katzenellenbogen).

- R. Jehiel Luria, A.B.D. Brisk (d. 1470).

- Miriam Spira (wife of R. Aaron Luria).

- R. Solomon Spira, A.B.D. Heilbron.

- Vergentin Hanna Treves (wife of R. Samuel Spira).

- R. Mattithiah Treves of Provence (1325–1387). See note 4.

- R. Joseph Treves, rabbi of Marseilles c. 1343.

- R. Johanan Treves (d. 1329).

- R. Abraham Treves.

- R. Mattityahu Treves.

- R. Joseph Treves.

- R. Jehiel Treves.

- Isaac be Meir. See note 5.

- Jochabed (married to Meir I, 1065–1135).

- Solomon ben Isaac, known in history as Rashi. See note 6.

- Sister of Simeon the Great [1005–1065], given name unknown.

- Isaac (960-1025).

- Abun (c.935-1000). Name unknown.

- Meshullam the Great (900–975). See note 7.

- Kalonymus (c. 875–925).

- Moses the Elder (c. 850–925).

- Name unknown.

- Name unknown.

- Name unknown.

- Natronai (715–790).

- Habibai (690–765).

- David (665–740).

- Hisdai (640–715).

- Bar Adai (615–680).

- Bustani (590–660). See note 8.

- Hanina (565–589).

- Huna Mar Huna (c.515–575).

Notes

1. A.B.D. is an acronym for Av Bet Din or Head of the Rabbinical Court which was empowered to render binding judicial rulings.

2. Jacob Emden, considered by many to be the most brilliant man of his generation, was involved in a dispute which split the Jewish community in half. He accused Jonathan Eybeshutz of being a follower of Sabatai Zvi, a self-proclaimed messiah. Eybeshutz's son was later discovered to have amulets which indicated that he (the

son) was in fact a follower of this false messiah.

3. A book, *The Unbroken Chain*, by Dr. Neil Rosenstein, traces the descendants of the Maharam of Padua. These include the Lord Mayor of London, Karl Marx, Felix Mendelsohn, Helena Rubinstein, and other notables.

4. Mattithiah Treves was appointed Chief Rabbi of Paris by King Charles V. He and his family were the only Jews of France exempted from wearing a yellow badge.

5. Isaac be Meir (translated, means Isaac the son of Meir) was known by the acronym RIBAM and was a leading commentator and annotator of the Bible.

6. Rashi is the foremost annotator of the Bible. His clarity of thought and analyses have never been surpassed. His work transcends Judaism, having been studied by Martin Luther.

7. Mehullam the Great and those names following were "exilarchs" (i.e., rulers in exile). A requirement for the post of exilarch was that the individual had to be a descendant of King David.

8. The Exilarch Bustani was compelled by the king to take a second, non-Jewish wife, so that he had two separate families, one Jewish, the other not.

55

What I Took after My Mother Died (2005)

- That watercolor of the San Francisco Bay, unabashedly and, I am sure, undeservedly bearing her signature.

- All her writings.

- A letter I wrote her when I was maybe around twelve telling her she was a great mom, the single thing she saved from my childhood.

56

What I Wanted (2005)

- That small cast iron frying pan seasoned by half a century of scrambled eggs cooked in butter that she either gave to someone else or threw away.

57

Letter Between My Parents, #3
(1962)

June, 1962

I have just finished sorting through some cartons in the attic in preparation for moving. How fortunate you are that you left all tangible memories behind. All around me I am surrounded by ghostly memories—aching reminders of other times, other places—letters you have written me when there was love in your heart—pictures of the children when they were babies—souvenirs of trips we have taken—bleached bones tossed up to face the glaring merciless sun of reality.

It is two o'clock in the morning—and the loneliness is smothering me. I know that nothing I can say will touch you in any way, penetrate the thick wall of bitterness you have constructed between us—but somehow it doesn't matter. I must write this.

For years I prayed that you would change, be more aware, show more sentiment. But how wrong I was. It wasn't really necessary for <u>you</u> to change—it was necessary for me to face reality. But what a terrible price I have had to pay. People can change—I have— but perhaps it takes something truly devastating to accomplish it—psychic trauma, or call it what you will. It takes something with such gigantic impact that it knocks the wind right out of you. I had an inkling of it when I was in the hospital with hepatitis—for awhile when I was so very sick—things seemed to assume different proportions of importance—I realized how many of the things I valued were false values. But the feelings left when I was forced back into the rat race too soon. But this agony that I have suffered for almost two years has given me plenty of time to shift and weigh my values. I would give anything to have a father for my children and a husband for myself. I have no false pride. Pride is a meaningless, shallow word. We only pass this way once—and it is such a short time—all the time getting shorter.

I always valued your mind, your standards, but I realize now that it wasn't enough. It was only when I lost you that I realized how much I had valued you as a man—a complete, whole man whom I loved very deeply—but unfortunately was never able to express.

I still love you—more deeply than ever. I have tried dating other men but it has been an empty farce—I compared them all to you and they all fell short.

I know what you are probably thinking—"It's too late"—but it isn't—I can prove it to you, that it isn't. People can change if the will is strong enough, if the incentive is there and if they are forced to face the truth as I have. Won't you please give me another chance. Meet me as if for the first time—meet me as I am now—not as I was when there was anger between us. I feel no anger, only pain. Please give us all this one more chance.

I will be in New York all week starting Monday, July 2—call me at Gr 3-9284—mornings or evenings. Please!

Lee

58

Letter Between My Parents, #4 (1963)

10/14/63

Lee:

Since you seem to have a short memory, I am going to quote from a couple of the letters you wrote me last year.

"I have hurt you—took your tenderest feelings and outraged them but this I swear—never consciously, never with any intent to hurt. It all stemmed from my blindness..."

"I pray that someday we can meet as friends, not so much for our sake, but for the sake of the children."

"For years I prayed that you would change, be more aware, show more sentiment—but how wrong I was. It wasn't really necessary for you to change—it was necessary for me to face reality. ...People can change. I have... It was only when I lost you that I realized how much I had valued you as a man—a complete, whole man whom I loved very deeply... "

And a good deal more horse-shit.

The reason it's horse-shit is not that the words aren't well chosen, or the sentiments fine and noble, or that the truth is not in it. The reason it's horse-shit is that the truth in your letters is not in you—that these letters are only another example of the dozens throughout our life together of exactly the same thing: you proceeding savagely and blindly to tear me to shreds, to insist on bullying through with some course of action that I could see clearly would lead to nothing but pain and trouble and regret, which I tried my God damnedest to persuade you to see, but about which you absolutely and flatly refused to entertain any discussion. And invariably, inevitably, monotonously—time after time after time, after it was all over and you had gotten your way and made yourself and everybody else so rotten miserable that just waking up in the morning was almost reason enough, for me at any rate, to slit my throat—then, when it was too late to undo or repair the harm, you'd magnanimously come forward and admit you'd been wrong, you hadn't "meant" it, and swore you had "changed."

Changed, shit. You never changed then, and you haven't changed now. I made it as clear to you as anyone with my limited powers of expression can possibly have done, that if you insisted on keeping up the torture you were putting me through, and drove me out of the house, you would have totally destroyed every last drop of a bond between us, and made it completely and totally impossible for me ever to return. While there was still time to do anything about it, as far as you were concerned all that was nothing, absolutely nothing. The only way you have ever been capable of understanding is by letting disaster happen—or worse, you actually help it along.

When I finally had to tell you—tell you, for Christ's sake!—that I had been fired from my job at the 4A's as a result of what your ministrations had done to me, you "didn't know!" Didn't know! If you'd had half an iota of decency, of concern, of sympathy, of care, or of any of the qualities you like to brag you're so God-damned good at, you'd have known not six months before, when I first began to know, but even before that. You sure as hell would have known at the time it happened.

If you'd had any of those qualities you'd have known that some people can take some things better than others can—and that there are some things I can't take very well at all. You'd have known just a little bit, at least, of the agonies of self-doubt and unworthiness I've been tortured by all my life. What I was too stupid and naïve to understand was that you could take so much sadistic pleasure in attacking me whenever I was down, and exactly where I was most vulnerable, with as sure an instinct for the jugular as a she-lion slaughtering an antelope...

Don't get the idea that I'm recounting all this obscene performance of yours with any illusion that any part of it will penetrate to your heart, or that it will have any effect at all on your evident determination to wreck me completely. I've been pretty stupid but nobody can be that stupid, not after the savage education you've given me.

I know exactly what is going to happen. I can see it as clearly as I saw all the things I tried to convince you would happen before, almost as clearly as if it had already happened and the whole stinking, rotten, useless, miserable mess that you've made of both our lives were all finished and done with and wiped out even of any living memory.

The only reason I'm doing this is to make it impossible for you, God damn you, ever to be able to say this time, "I didn't know." I want you to know clearly and unmistakably what you're doing before you do it. I want to rub your nose in it so hard you can never forget it as long as you live. Because then, when you've done it, I want you to have to live with your conscience, if there is any such thing in you.

So read these facts carefully, and digest them thoroughly with all their implications—not for me, you bitch, because as far as I'm concerned my life is clearly over and done with—but for you and the children. Get them fixed firmly and clearly in your mind.

1. *If you keep on your present course of harassing me, whether you go through with the court threat or not, some time within the next several months or a year my work will have deteriorated far enough to that the bvi authorities will no longer be able to mistake it, and I will get another invitation to "resign."*

2. *Even if you leave me completely alone, there is still a question of whether I will be able any longer to regain enough morale to pull myself out eventually. This is, however, the <u>only</u> remaining chance.*

3. *If you go through with the court threat, I am not going to respond. I <u>cannot</u> endure the indignity and humiliation.*

4. *If you then send the goons for me, I will have no choice left but to quit the job. It would be utterly impossible for me to function at it even if they'd let me, which is pretty damn unlikely.*

5. *Whenever you and the goons and the shysters—you*

deserve each other!—are finished with me, and have taken from me whatever you are capable of taking, I will try to survive as long as I can, for as long as whatever you leave me holds out.

6. *When that runs out I'll take an overdose of sleeping tablets or carbon monoxide, because by that time what the shit reason will there be to do anything else?*

7. *What brings us back to your heart-rending letters—because then I can just see you and hear you saying it, as you've always said it—"I didn't know—never consciously, never with any intent to hurt—nothing I have done was through malice— people can change, I have—we only pass this way once, and it is such a short time, and the time is getting shorter—it was only when I had lost you that I realized how much I valued you... "*

To which I say bullshit. If you're going to have your heart cut out anyway, I and any man would a thousand times rather have it done honestly with malice, than hypocritically with crocodile tears.

A.

59

An Abbreviated Accounting of My History with Men

START BY HAVING A CRAZY MAN FOR A FATHER, someone who leaves and never looks back and when you find him decades later, when you see how weird and limited and damaged he is, you wonder how that would have worked anyway, if he'd stayed, would you have been any better off because either way—here or gone—you never were going to feel protected and guarded and cherished by this first man, never were going to be daddy's little girl, never would have had a beautiful first love, never would be able to carry a sense of unquestioned girl-loved-by-boy value into the world and without even realizing, you form a rooted belief about what men are like and what to expect from them.

L.
Earlier than most get totally boy crazy to the exclusion of almost anything else and find a serious boyfriend, a guy who is remote, taciturn, withholding, and older, because to you all that seems strong and mysterious and deep and you stay with him for years even though he will eventually lie and cheat and let you down, all the while holding onto you so fiercely.

R.
Zero in on someone pretty quickly once you get to college because the thought of anything else other than marriage after graduation never even occurs to you, the only thing on your mind is to have fun so you find someone you can party with and, though you only see this to be beyond embarrassing in retrospect, you have the deep-down sense that you have the power here, just like you learned from your mother, you are in charge and you actually believe he's lucky to have you because that's how you were trained to feel, so you can go on and be your unexamined self, never mind about stupid stuff like compatibility or values or differences or the future or who the hell is he anyway, don't pay attention to those shadows out the corner of your eye, just move along and get married, sleepwalk through the first years of marriage, have two children because

that's what you do, right?, feel bored and mildly depressed but since you never have known how to look at yourself and the thought doesn't even occur to you anyway, rack up the years in some semi-conscious state, knowing full well you do not have what it takes to make yourself a different life, all the while having the unsettled feeling that it's all wrong.

P.

Maybe it's only boredom that pushes you but you begin to think maybe you can *do* something, maybe there is more in the world for you and it's psychology you decide on, totally missing the most obvious reasons why, but even so, it moves you out of your quotidian life, moves you out and threatens to unsettle that life because you can't stay as deeply denied as you have been, you can see you need something more or at least something different and, since no way you have the courage to make that happen yourself and, because you can't let go of one life preserver until you have another to grab onto, you meet someone else, someone that promises to give you all you didn't have before, like sparkle and wit and sophistication, a life of cocktail parties and wine from France and repartee, all Nick and Nora Charles, the things that look so good to you on paper, all the while ignoring the early cautionary signs you could have noticed but what you did instead was file them away and contort them into things you could actually admire like maybe the petulant demand for attention was somehow honest and emotionally open but when the party guests leave and it's just the two of you, there's anger and steely cold and criticism and both of you behaving badly, you unwittingly, unconsciously reverting right back to the ugly behavior you saw in your mother and you can see that it should have only been a fling at most anyway but now you are on the train and no way you are jumping off so you stay in your defensive, shut-down place and wait till he decides he needs more than you are willing to give and leaves.

C.

You give lip service to being single and how you're in no hurry but you flirt and seduce and are on the look-out, not really considering what you might get out of some real time alone so when you meet this new guy and feel that lusty jolt, you let yourself be swept off your feet, bedazzled and pursued hard, being flown first class here and there, all the while, once again, unable to totally ignore the glaring, sky-high, red neon-lettered warning signs, all that slippery ma-nipulation and thinly veiled narcissism that could be seen from outer space, all pointing to disaster but he's like no one you've ever met before, and even though, truth be told, you're not much better than a high-class whore, and that all the people who know you are wondering what the hell is she thinking, you tell yourself you know better, this is a brave choice and no one knows more than the people in a relationship, right?, besides you are kind of stuck in your life and no way you have it in you to shake things up on your own so why not move across the country to a place you've barely heard of with this man who no one in your life gets, and truthfully you don't either, but cross your fingers and leap because hell, you're already down the road of marriage loser, that boat has sailed, what's one more, so no surprise it ends in the ugly way any fool could have predicted.

W.

Because you're older and burned and feeling like it would be good to live a braver life anyway—after all it's a bit unseemly for a nearly fifty-year-old to be so boy-crazy—you decide to actually commit to that life, to drop the search and settle into yourself. It actually does feel good, you start to know it, when you buy your own small place, with only your name on the mortgage, and it's you and your cat. You feel the beginnings of strong. Maybe you are a full person— you've got this career and your own place and a circle of friends and you begin to have a sense of enough. And then Donna calls. She says you have to meet this guy, he's wonderful. You're reluctant and so new at this feeling whole in yourself, but this is Donna and you saved her and she saved you and if she says he's wonderful, he must be. So you agree, yes, when he's out here you'll meet him, have dinner, go for a hike, and, bless her heart, she's right. He's such a nice man, someone you would trust with your life and even though you don't feel that instant zingy charge, and in spite of the fact he's obviously smitten which always had been the number one allure, you have to talk yourself into the next time and the time after. But after a while you start to notice how in the space where your need had been, there is now space to really know who he is and how it might work, this time letting go of the inevitability you always attached yourself to before, feeling like you had no choice but to be swept along. This time you think and talk and wonder and see that by microscopic increments there is a place in you that is thawing and releasing and loving, a place so embryonic and new, so unused to the sunlight that it—this heart of yours—it needs this kind of patience and tolerance and no bullshit honesty and you see so clearly that you can't have a man—this man—unless you are a woman, not your mother's fucked-up version of a woman but the kind which, finally, at this late age, you are just starting to be. My dear Donna was so right because we did have those handful of beautiful years that just might have turned into a lifetime or maybe not but we can't know because he died.

60

Searching for Equanimity

I NEVER HESITATE TO TELL THE STORY ABOUT THE black coat. Or the cruise. Or the Academy Awards. Or about the time she invited my niece, then maybe nine or ten years old, to bring a friend for a fancy day in the city: theater and dinner. My niece chose to bring her favorite babysitter and they set out for this supposed fun time. At some point in the middle of the play, my mother got up, in the dark, not at intermission, with no explanation, without a single word, and left. She just left. She left her seat and she left the theater. I wouldn't know what to do if I were in their shoes and how do you imagine a pre-cellphone ten-year-old and her teenage babysitter could figure it out, there in the city on their own.

Or there was the time we gathered for my daughter's college graduation. Picture a perfect early summer Seattle day, everything sparkly and shiny new. See us walking along the boardwalk on our way to a waterside restaurant to celebrate, a big boisterous crew of us. There is my mother walking between my two girls, me several yards behind. I'm too far away to hear what they are talking about but close enough to see my girls as they slowly lower their heads, down and down until they are literally hanging. By the time I hustle up close enough to hear, she is saying something like *how do you think it makes me feel when I see you being so nice to your mother, I mean what about me, why does she get all the attention?*

There's no end to these stories.

I never hesitate to tell these stories. In fact, I'm eager to tell them. I look for any opening to squeeze one into a conversation, sometimes finding only the vaguest connection to the topic at hand. And if the subject of narcissism comes up I hop right in, tell a story or two, and invariably end up walking away with the prize. Okay, they say, you win. No one can top the stories about my mother.

On the surface it must appear I hold the deluded idea it reflects well on me, winning this dubious prize. Maybe it's because I imagine some mental calculation going on for my audience, like wow, how did *she* manage to be so healthy with a mother like that? Or maybe it's a strategic end-run around my own failures, like no wonder she's been less than successful in the romance department with *her* for a mother. Yes, but as unflattering as those motives might be, I'm afraid it's even worse. In my come-to-Jesus meetings with myself, I see this need to flaunt my psycho mother for what it is: my own narcissism. (This horrifying conclusion—choke on it though I will—I promise to get back to.)

Now, though, it's about this: after the dinner guests have gone, or on her birthday, or on the anniversary of her death—or anytime that I really stop to truly reflect, I think of how heartbreakingly small she was, how weird and ridiculous her hair had become, all frizzed and brittle. I think about how brutal her family must have been and how brave she was to make such a different life for herself so far from her original home. I think about the picture I have of her as maybe a teenager in mid-somersault, all joy and possibility. I think about how bare she was about her loneliness and her need.

This is where I live—somewhere smack between pity and rage, between empathy and indictment. And as hard as I look, I still can't find a place to rest between mercy and pain.

61

Mother, Where Can I Rest?

MARY HAS BEEN MY CLIENT FOR AROUND THREE years. It's a persistent theme for her, the anger she has for her mother. Mary is filled with rage.

She says, "Every word out of the bitch's mouth is some criticism or other. Why does she have to comment on every stupid little thing? She's never once said she was proud of me, would that kill her, just once?"

Mary has tried everything: confronting, arguing, tears, avoidance, silence. She has gone into her bedroom closet, pushed her face into the hanging clothes, and screamed her throat ragged.

I say, "What is this anger doing for you, Mary? It's true, your mother's never going to change and your anger is totally justified. But now, here and now, what does this anger accomplish? How is it helping you and what would be hard about letting it go?"

I say, "Mary, this anger is poisoning you and only you. For your own sake, find a way to let it go."

In my first session with Dan he tells me something of his childhood, how his father was his role model, so hard-working and strong. Dan only saw him for a couple of hours on the weekends, his hard work and all, and he understood why his father needed to drink. The pressure. So much responsibility. Yes, he got irritable (no, not mean) and Dan knew better than to ask if he were coming to his baseball game.

I say, "Did you feel loved by him?"

We were both aware of the time it took to answer this question until he finally said...

"Sure, yes. I'm sure I must have."

In almost every session there was a story about his father, or at least some oblique reference. His father, who had for all his young life, pitted Dan against his older, better, smarter, more-loved brother. His father who has met Dan's own son—now nine years old—exactly twice. His father who picked the day of his mother's cancer diagnosis to ask for a divorce. Sometimes I ask Dan how he feels about the whole thing.

"Fine," he says, "Fine. I don't see what good it does to... "

"To what?" I ask.

"You know," he says. "It's in the past. I know he was doing the best he could." When I ask him how he feels, what I mean is *Don't you feel angry? Aren't you furious? Don't you have decades of roiling wrath? Don't you know, Dan, that it will poison you, this unexpressed rage? Can't you see how it seeps out anyway, all the passive-aggressive shit you pull with your wife? … You deserve these feelings, Dan. They are righteous.*

And this is where I am. Bouncing back and forth between Mary and Dan, forever hoping to at last find a place of equanimity, some place where I can finally plant my flag. When my mother was alive it was even worse, the bouncing. Here's how it went: I get home after seeing her and I spend some number of days decompressing. I tell my friends all the insane stories, all the ways she drove me to the brink. I get in bed at 6:30 P.M., eat bags of potato chips, and watch a shitload of dumb TV. It's my own special cleanse. Then maybe a week later I see a woman at a bus stop, a string bag of groceries on her lap, and my heart breaks just a little. She looks somehow forsaken. Her children don't call her, I think. She lives alone. She is old. She is tired. Her body aches. And then, soon, I think about my mother. I was so harsh with her. Why did I have to be so cold and withholding? She's tragic, not evil, for chrissake! Have some compassion, or pity, at least! How empty she must feel to behave the way she does. I can only guess how she was damaged but it's clear she was. *I* must be the monster to carry so much anger against such a pitiful soul. I thaw. I melt. I'll call her tonight. I'll send her a nice card. I will change. And if I have zero contact with her—no phone call, no visit, no communication of any kind—I can pretty much stay there in a place of charity. Until. Truly it takes maybe eight minutes in person or three sentences on the phone and I'm back. Twisted gut and hardened heart. It takes just that long to annihilate whatever melting may have happened.

Now that she's dead there's less bouncing, of course. In fact I only feel the merest echoes of anger. Mostly I reside in a place of mercy and compassion. I am relieved. I am unburdened. So very, very sad. How fuckingly hard it was to love her. How sorely I wanted to.

62

Wish List

I HAVE A FAMILY THAT HAD DINNER TOGETHER every night.

I have bohemian parents who took me out of school for weeks at a time just because.

I have three older brothers and one younger sister.

I have overindulgent parents.

I have an aunt who taught me how to smoke and swear.

I have parents who bicker.

I have aunts and uncles and cousins who lived on the same block as me.

I have a mother who's more like a sister to me.

I have a family that fought at the dinner table with shouting and name-calling and door-slamming.

I have a black sheep cousin.

I have a dying grandmother.

I have parents who are bored with each other.

I have relatives in the Old Country.

I have a vacation cottage in Maine that's been in the family for five generations.

I have family reunions every year.

I have parents who are brave enough to be mad at me.

I have a grouchy grandfather who lived with us my whole childhood.

I have my father's dog tags and war medals.

I have six nieces and three nephews.

I have a grandmother who taught me how to sew and make peach pie and play bridge.

I have a family home I return to every year where my old bedroom still has my stuffed animals on the bed and my Beatles poster on the wall.

I have an eccentric uncle.

I have a father who always called me Daddy's Little Girl.

I have a quilt my grandmother made for me when I was born, faded and stained and worn with love and age.

I have a henpecked father.

I have annoying cousins.

I have a family that sings and dances together.

I have parents who turn to me for help because my brother seems to have gone off the deep end.

I have a twin sister.

I have a grandfather who took me deep sea fishing off Cape Cod every summer.

I have a big, embracing, frustrating, effortless, tussling, bountiful, affectionate, annoying, blessed, abundant, regular, ordinary, boring, full of family-ness family.

63

Terminal (2002)

S HE SAYS JUST DROP ME AT THE CURB AND I SAY
NO, no I'll park and come find you but it's only
something you say and really we both wanted the
visit over with. Me, I'd reached my limit about five
minutes after she arrived three days earlier. The rest
of the weekend I spent monitoring myself: *smile; try
not to react; be patient; don't hold your face in that tight,
cold way; be kind; breathe, don't forget to fucking breathe.*

It's only once I pull up to the curb at Departures
that we start in with the stuff you say at times like this:
*It was so great to see you, I had a wonderful time, when can
we do this again.* Which somehow makes it all worse.
Because those few minutes, right before she gets out

of the car, those few minutes are our blessed chance to finally say it: how much we've hurt each other, how angry and bewildered we've been, how wrong we were as mother and daughter. This is our chance, maybe our last chance, after nearly six decades.

But no, once again, no. She gets out of the car, I fetch her suitcase from the trunk, we hug, and she walks through the revolving door and into the terminal. I might never forget this feeling, watching her walk away from me. She is impossibly small and her smallness is so achingly sad. There is burden in the folding in of her shoulders and shame in the downward tilt of her head. Her arms hang with the weight of resignation and failure. Her walk is a shuffle of despair. I could be wrong, of course. She could be grinning and hopeful. She could be flush and content and maybe it's merely my own sorrow I feel.

There *is* something about watching someone walk away from you. On my refrigerator is a photograph of my grandson at the beach the winter he was two. He's bundled in down and boots and hat and mittens, walking toward the ocean, also away from me. In the mix of feelings I have looking at the picture is also sadness. Maybe the heartbreaking truth of his innocence and vulnerability is easier to access without seeing his face. But with him there is also this: his electric blue eyes, that impossible dimple high on his left cheek, his trouble with Rs and Ls. There's how excited he is to play with his bulldozer in the sand and imagining what he sees when he looks out over the Pacific Ocean and there is my certain lifetime of loving him.

I can't drive away.

I run in after her and throw myself at her feet, my arms tight around her ankles. We are shattered and open. We are full of forgiveness and mercy. Mom. Mommy.

Or, she drops to the floor right there in the airport, dead, a swift and final stroke or maybe a heart attack and finally I am free.

64

Letter Between My Parents, #5
(1966)

2/7/66

August—

This will be the last communication you will ever receive from me. I will no longer expose myself to the abusive filth of your sick mind. In case your memory is vague about the horrible things you have written or you were in an alcoholic stupor at the time I can send you copies. In the future if you have anything to say, say it to my lawyer.

I trusted your integrity when you told me those lies about waiting to hear about your contract renewal—did without any support money at all, and then put up with your arbitrary reduction of the amount to exactly half—no decent explanation—nothing. You left me no alternative but to restart legal action.

How dare you talk about a reasonable compromise. Exactly what is your idea of a "reasonable compromise"—that you reduce the alimony to $50 a week and we assume the full obligation of educating the girls—or are you willing to be reasonable. I will wait a week to hear your offer—and I promise to be reasonable about it—and dismiss my legal rights. If however, at the end of the week I have no longer heard from you, I wash my hands of the whole thing and from then on my attorney handles it. Liz will be 19 in March. Your obligation will end soon enough. At least do something for them...

You ask for a "reasonable compromise," quoting your words. Let's hear it.

L.

65

Letter Between My Parents, #6 (1966)

2/17/66

Let me remind you of some <u>facts</u>—facts that have brought this whole situation about, and are going to determine whatever happens in the future.

I was the injured party, not you. You were the one who told me to get out, not I who deserted you. It took several years for me to get the message but I finally got it.

I told you repeatedly that if I ever left I wasn't coming back. Yet for a year or two after I left you tried to persuade me to come back... .

After I left, and while you were still acting more or less reasonably and considerately, I did more to cooperate with you than any court would ever have required... This was all far more than I could afford, with the result that every month, every year, I was going steadily deeper into the hole.

Never after I left (or before, for that matter) did I discuss a word of our relationship with anyone else. People who to this day you think are friends of yours would tell me they thought it was about time I got rid of you, that they didn't understand how I could have stomached you for as long as I did, and every time I changed the subject. But you, you couldn't wait to go around and start slandering me. And of all the colossal lies you could have chosen, to tell people I was impotent! There are more than thirty women who know otherwise. To translate the fact that you made yourself personally and sexually repulsive to me into my impotence has got to be one of the most stupefying feats of mental acrobatics of all time. But I don't care half as much about that as about the breach of faith, in talking behind my back at all.

When I phoned you from out of town, you deliberately lied to me about the terms of the decree, you told me the amount of support. I asked if there was anything else. You said no, nothing else but $100 a week support. I asked again and again and you said no. Christ knows that after the experience with your goons I shouldn't have been so stupid and gullible as to *believe you. But I somehow couldn't get it into my head that you would actually be capable of telling, to my face, a lie that bald and flagrant. Once again, though, you taught me the hard way.*

I came back <u>only</u> because of your lie. If you had been honest, I would not have come back at all. I would rather have taken an overdose of sleeping pills or an exhaust pipe than knowingly put my neck into that vise. You've brought me to the brink of suicide more than once, and one of the closest was when I opened the decree and discovered a little more about your nature.

If they choose to fire me I have no severance protection beyond what they feel in the goodness of their hearts they'd like to throw me. They can kick me out without notice and without a nickel any time they choose, and I will have no claim and no recourse.

If I had absolutely no recreation and relaxation— and above all escape—these past two or three years, I'd have gone under long ago. The <u>only</u> things that have kept me alive this long and have kept me from going any farther downhill than I have, are (1) sex (2) golf (3) alcohol, and (4) music and books—in that order. If I were permanently deprived of any one of these outlets, these opportunities to forget your hooks buried in my flesh, to forget the job, to lose myself for a little while in a world where vampires aren't sucking my blood and vultures aren't tearing at my liver, then screw the whole shit-stinking mess. I tell *you once again—and don't kid yourself that this is empty talk, any more than the things I've told you plainly in the past have been—if you deprive me of these, the only reasons left that have made it possible for me to survive as long as I have, then I'm going to finish the whole stinking thing with the exhaust pipe. You think I'm bluffing? Just remember that every time you've thought so in the past you've discovered that I wasn't.*

Alcohol, music and books are no great problem, because they don't cost much. But sex and golf do cost money. If I could get laid two or three times a week without the dinners, motel rooms and other costs that often go with it, I'd do so. If I could play golf in decent surroundings, surroundings that befit my exalted positions, without spending money, I'd do it.

What I spend on broads and golf, if you had sense enough to realize it, is as much for your benefit as mine. Without money for broads and golf there wouldn't be any money period—for me, for you, for anything. The twenty bucks it may cost me to get laid tonight is what makes it possible for me to show up in the office and struggle through the day tomorrow.

The only question, therefore, from your point of view, is this: is it your purpose to do me as much harm as possible? If it is, you're in control. All you have to do is go to court. That will finish off whatever is left of my earning power. If you demand your last ounce of flesh it will put me in jail as well. Then the first chance

I get I'll commit suicide. But I promise you, I'll do it in a way that will ruin your life as you have ruined mine, that will make you wish as long as you live that you had never been born.

I am completely in sympathy with the support provision. I demonstrated that by action not just words, from the time I left until you started double-crossing me. But aside from the punitive amounts that are involved, I resent being required by court decree to pay for education—especially without having any voice whatever in determining how much is to be spent on it! What court required my father to send me to college? Only about half of all high school graduates enter college, and a lot of them are on reduced tuition, or on loans for them to repay after graduation, or in tuition-free schools. What court required the parents of the other to send them to college, and give them no voice in what it costs?

Do you <u>really</u> want to see the kids properly educated? If you do, do you really think tearing me down with this kind of court decree is the way to do it... wouldn't you have been smarter to limit the decree to a burden I could carry without collapsing under it, and rely on my decency and humanity to do everything in my power beyond that? Don't you think I would have been <u>able</u> to do a great deal more that way? Don't you think I would have been vastly more <u>willing</u>?

Think all this over carefully. Forget the fantasies, the way you might wish things could be. Concentrate on the _actual alternative_. Imagine how each one would _actually_ affect your life and the kids'. Remember that once you take a step there's no undoing it, once you commit yourself to one fork or the other you're stuck with it.

Support at $5,200 a year as given in the decree is almost exactly one-third of my net income. By any reasonable standard that's more than enough of a burden for any man to carry as a legal requirement. I cannot only live with it, I'll be glad to live with it. But only if the two other axes you hold over my neck—the provision on education and insurance— are neutralized in some way that frees me from the constant threat that anytime you may choose to take into your head you can swing the axe. Unless I'm free of that threat there's no reason to make any effort at all. With that threat removed, I can at least try to rebuild my life.

A.

66

Chasing My Father
(1947 to present)

A<small>ND THEN THERE'S MY FATHER. M</small>Y DEAD, ANGRY
father who once was my hero. I don't drag out
stories about *him* at dinner parties. I don't talk about
him and roll my eyes. I don't feel the tug of guilt I do
when I'm up on my high horse pontificating about
narcissism and how you can't hold a candle to my
mother, just go ahead and try. He's at least as culpable
and definitely as diagnosable and if I wanted to, I'd
have plenty to say. Until I found the letters I'd written
him, I had not remembered my pitiful promise—that
I would do my best to forget all about him.

* * *

A client tells me about all the times she moved as a kid. She says, "I've been chasing my father my whole life." It takes longer than usual for either of us to say anything. I'm trying what is impossible so she won't notice. Both of us are caught off guard.

With my mother there were all those stories. All the disappointments and pull-your-hair-out frustrations and maddening habits and infuriating interactions. I could go on and on. With him I have this: the smell of white shirts after a day in the city; Chopin on the black piano; a sense of his presence in the basement building furniture. Darkness and absence.

My client thought she was only talking about geography. Then we sat in that dangerous silence, me unable to keep the flush off my face, both of us hijacked by the weight of it all.

67

My Parents' Marriage

NOT LONG AGO I FOUND SOME OLD 8MM MOVIE film that I didn't even know I had and have no idea how I even came to have it. One reel. One reel that I had transferred to disc that same day and tapped my foot impatiently until I could pick it up and rush home so I could sit down to watch. Imagine the excited anticipation. It could be anything. It could be important. It could be the answer.

In my own life, in the recesses of my own brain, I have somehow duplicated the complete void of facts and memories and information that so frustrated me with my family. My friend Donna remembers everything. It's mind-boggling. "You were wearing that red sweater and we were in your rec room with Bobby, remember?" Uh, no. Sometimes when she recounts a childhood incident I get a faint impression, a picture so overexposed that I can barely make out the shapes but that's about it. It's comforting, though, hearing her talk about experiences we had. It's reassuring. I have a witness. I was there, having a life.

The tape is four minutes long. Black and white and soundless, except for the crackles of old movie film. Jerky motion, two people, it looks like on a mountain, a wilderness. Smoky Mountain, Tennessee. How do I know this? A woman, my mother, points across the valley. And a little girl, me, under five probably because there is no sign of my younger sister. It had to be my father holding the camera. Once again he is out of sight. My parents are on this trip together, we are on this trip together, yet he is absent from the picture.

What happened with their marriage? In my work I've been witness to hundreds of marriages that have disintegrated or downright exploded. I think the jury's in on this: it's fucking hard to navigate a marriage over time and maintain respect and goodwill, let alone loving feelings. And the dynamic between people can be so complex. One of the occupational hazards (read: benefits) of my work is to always see both sides. There's no villain here, no victim, I'm quick to say. It's a dance.

But what happened with my parents?

I cannot access a single memory of them together. There's not one scene I can reproduce. I have my sense of him and my sense of her. And I know what it feels like to be in a relationship with each of them. And those relationships are less than healthy.

Here's my best guess: They met when they were young, she very young, probably a teenager still. They were both fractured from their families. Even though they both came from Jewish homes they, for I don't know what reason, each wanted to deny their heritage. To erase it altogether. My hunch is that marrying was a bold, romantic, fuck-you statement to their families. I only have his early letters but, oh my, the passion. Here was an enamored man imagining the paradise of their first apartment. This is how he saw her: *understanding, more or less tolerant, a bit flip, even tart, and loving—above all, loving.*

I have no information about what that early time was like for my mother, how she felt about him. I have that one picture of them sitting in the grass and they look peaceful and sweet and in love. Later, after he had left, what I remember is her frequent reference to how brilliant he was, that he scored the highest score ever registered on some test somewhere; that he got into Cornell at fourteen or eight or some ridiculously young age. I have no idea if any of that is true. Maybe so, but it could be another badge of honor that my mother flashed in her endless displays of grandiosity.

Here's what I actually know about each of them from first-hand experience:

Him: Even though my parents were together for the first ten years of my life, all I have is a feeling of absence. That has to mean something about him, doesn't it? The first actual memory I have is the goodbye lunch in the city. I haven't even thought about this part till recently but what must it have been like for me to get back on that train and go home after my father tells me he doesn't want to see me again, that it's just too hard for him. As an adult I can make plenty of conclusions about him based on that incident alone: selfish, infantile, narcissistic, unloving, complete dick. Later, when we would meet again as adults, I had a little more information to form a picture of who he was. This was a man who was seething with the most vicious and cruel sentiment toward my mother after they separated; refused to speak to his second wife, to whom he was clearly attached, for a span of two years; was quick to indignation over small slights; found himself in petty legal battles; reacted with violent defensiveness when I asked him to explain what had happened; and stubbornly refused to reach across the divide between him and his children.

Her: I have endless examples of how painfully difficult my mother could be. Leaving aside the mothering parts, I was witness to how she was in her two subsequent marriages. And it was not pretty. She was demeaning and emasculating even though (maybe, in fact, *because*) these two men clearly worshipped and adored her. They were like little puppies yapping at her ankles, puppies she would brusquely swat away and then suffer guilt and remorse over her treatment of these "good men," as she would call them. Almost unbearable to observe. And I heard her so many times vow to be different, to appreciate the man in her life, to be kind. This had to be much of the torture of her last years, after the death of her last husband—all the regret and guilt and squandered opportunity. She was controlling, demeaning, and contemptuous and I was witness to this cycle of bad behavior followed by remorse more times than I can count. It's not easy to admit this but I have had to keep a close eye on this same tendency in my marriages. I've been blessed with keen observational skills, a valuable trait in my profession, for sure. I can discern even the slightest change in tone or a microscopic facial tic. But I have also been cursed with the impulse to take that laser focus and zone in on any shortcoming, any imperfection, any minute evidence of human frailty. This is my inheritance. Yes, I have spent decades trying to exorcise this demon trait and, blessedly, I've made good progress. Still, at times the judgment rises like bile and I have to try my damndest to choke it back.

* * *

The little time I had with my father as an adult—along
with information from his second wife—leads me to
conclude that he felt fairly anchored in his defensive,
righteous, and unapologetic stance. His wife told me
that she knew he felt bad about his relationship with his
children but I saw none of that struggle myself, nor in
fact did she. She just wanted it to be true. In contrast,
my mother had a real and mighty internal battle going
on. She was cursed with a consciousness about her bad
behavior but a seeming compulsion to go right on with it.
She was tortured. And because of her transparent struggle, the empathy scale tips in her direction in my mind.

The old story I'd created about my father and
me—how we were so close, so connected, soul-
mates—just didn't work any more. Not after I'd had
real, in-person interaction with him. Not after such
an unmitigated disillusionment. As for my mother,
all the stories I had about her were reinforced time
and time and time again. So in the years since I've
struggled: Was there a villain in this family drama?
How do I allot the pity? Which one of them should
I claim and which should I reject? I can't begin to
know how to quantify the lunacy. I think of my father,
how he abandoned us and how unwilling he was to
make amends. How apparent it was that we meant
so little to him. On the other hand, when I read
those vile letters between my parents it's not hard

for me to understand his anger toward her. So many times I was witness to my mother's demeaning and manipulative behavior toward the men in her life and it was beyond cringe-worthy. I sympathize with you, father. And then I think about my mother and it's one infuriating interaction after another—that's where I go first. There's been no single person in my life so capable of bringing me to my knees in a state of anger, despair, and utter desolation. On the other hand, she was the one who taught my Brownie troop how to make hospital corners. She was the one who sewed up Halloween costumes and made full, fabulous wardrobes for my dolls. She was the one who, as a single woman, managed to send both her daughters to private colleges. And she was a model of a woman out in the world taking care of business, unconstrained by any societal norms or conventions.

As a child I opted for the absent one and developed a bond that I can see now was a transmutation, a fiction I'd created in order to feel some semblance of secure attachment. I turned his abandonment into a symbol of stolid, cool-headed strength. She was the crazy one. He was my invisible savior.

This all might have been at some level predestined in that I physically more resemble my father and my sister more resembles my mother. So there might have been some genetic predisposition to line up behind one parent or the other. Genetic or not, I not only physically resemble my father more, but in my younger life

I also adopted traits I imagined he had. My father and I, we are both dark, enigmatic, and unconventional.

I don't fault my young self for blindly opting for my father. Why not? All children crave secure attachment; it's a desire that's felt as life or death. It's just too scary to know that both of your parents are unstable. These parents of ours are the ones who feed us and shelter us. Our little lives depend on them, literally. It's no wonder some of us make stories out of any fragments, real or imagined, to reassure us that yes, someone is here for me; someone loves me; someone will take care of me so I will not die.

What I am saying though, is that until I came face to face with the man who was my father, I had a very rigid and unsophisticated story about my parents. In fact it was strikingly binary: she's bad; he's good. In the decades since, I've been on a kind of evaluative seesaw, like this:

He was cold-hearted and mentally unstable.

But she was manipulative and needy beyond needy.

But it took courage for him to extract himself from the double bind machinations she so routinely employed.

But she single-handedly parented us without any support.

But he was mentally ill; it was all beyond his control.

But she had to have suffered some major childhood trauma.

And on and on and on.
So: I believe them both.
I pity them both.
I blame them both.
I so wish I could say I love them both.

68

Something I Used to Be Good at but Am Not So Good at Anymore

• Resilience.

69

Some Issues That Are Hard for a Child of Narcissists to Sort Out

I DO MY BEST TO AVOID TREATING PEOPLE WITH Narcissistic Personality Disorder. Other therapists have way more patience, way less sensitivity. Early in my career it was nearly opaque to me but I know now that it's too damn close to home for me to be of any use. I'm just not the right person for that gig. I wish I could say that I've deactivated those buttons entirely, that my sensitivity is history. Sadly, it ain't so.

Here's the diagnostic criteria for Narcissistic Personality Disorder according to *The Diagnostic and Statistical Manual of Mental Disorders (DSM-IV)*:

A pervasive pattern of grandiosity (in fantasy or behavior), need for admiration, and lack of empathy, beginning by early adulthood and present in a variety of contexts, as indicated by five (or more) of the following:

1. Has a grandiose sense of self-importance (e.g., exaggerates achievements and talents, expects to be recognized as superior without commensurate achievements).

2. Is preoccupied with fantasies of unlimited success, power, brilliance, beauty, or ideal love.

3. Believes that he or she is "special" and unique and can only be understood by, or should associate with, other special or high-status people (or institutions).

4. Requires excessive admiration.

5. Has a sense of entitlement, i.e., unreasonable expectations of especially favorable treatment or automatic compliance with his or her expectations.

6. Is interpersonally exploitative, i.e., takes advantage of others to achieve his or her own ends.

7. Lacks empathy: is unwilling to recognize or identify with the feelings and needs of others.

8. Is often envious of others or believes that others are envious of him or her.

9. Shows arrogant, haughty behaviors or attitudes.

Here are some major challenges for me, child of two diagnosable narcissists:

1. Attention: A psychic once told me that I have a very ambivalent relationship with the concept of attention. Maybe everyone does so that would make it an easy rabbit to pull out of a would-be psychic hat. Even so, it's not only true about me—it's *super* true. I like being the center of attention. In fact I like it quite a lot. But it has to happen in a kind of sly way, craftily, it's not like I'm asking for it, I promise. And then once I'm in the spotlight I deflect and squirm like I'm wearing a sweater three sizes too small. There's no pleasing me. Here's a brief story about my mother and attention: she was visiting me and I invited a friend over to have dinner with us, someone with whom I had taken a recent trip. Everything is going fine at the table, eating and talking, and then I remember I have photos from the trip so I bring them out to show my friend. About four pictures in my mother gets up from the table without a word and disappears. Twenty minutes later I find her in my guestroom, lying on the bed with all the lights off. So I

do not know how the fuck to make peace with this matter of attention.

2. Compliments: It's automatic: whenever I get a compliment, I have a knee-jerk response, something like: *This old thing, I got it years ago—on sale.* I suspect it's part braggadocio: I'm so wily, so smart, I know how to game the system. But there's more to this particular variety of deflection. I cannot accept the compliment because I don't deserve it. And, more importantly, I don't want you to think that I believe I deserve it. Reality doesn't really factor in here. Facts don't matter a whit. The calculus is deeply embedded: accepting a compliment = I deserve the compliment = I think I'm all that = I am a narcissist.

3. Pride: I don't know, isn't the pride you feel in someone else always bloodsucking? My mother told me she was proud of me countless times, some of which was warranted, some not so much. But I remember how it felt, how often my mother would drag me out to play piano for her guests or pull out a report card or invent some accomplishment and puff herself up and say *Well, I must have done* something *right*. Which, fuck you, I never knew what to do with that. It always felt like giving and taking at the same time.

So we're really talking about you, again, always, still, mom. Me as mirror, you as star.

The upshot of this is that I am supremely careful about the use of that word. Pride. There's probably not an hour that goes by that I don't feel proud of my kids in some way or other. And just like the well-worn phrase goes, I swell with that feeling. But what is that swelling but a puffing myself up, making myself big somehow. It all feels so self-serving to me that I kind of choke on it when I say, "I'm so proud of you, daughter." I take a microscope to my intentions, submit them to some kind of purity test, reassure myself that I am taking no credit. Poor kids.

4. Expressing Need: I have no idea how much personal information to share with my adult children. And by personal information I mostly mean my struggles and my pains. How much to lean on them. My sister and I were so burdened by our mother's neediness, by the sack of high-octane shit she could not wait to unload on us. And, you gotta give it to her, she was open in ways most parents, actually most people, are not. Way open. She'd tell anyone—the bank teller, the barista, the bus driver—how her medication isn't

working and she has bloody diarrhea and how no one appreciates her. My fallback position with my kids is to be practically mute. If asked, I will tell but I bend way over backward to avoid anything in the neighborhood of neediness. Is that the right tack to take? I doubt it.

5. Parenting: I don't have a clue about what it is to be a good mother and whether or not I've come anywhere close.

6. Gifts: Is there a price tag attached to every gift, every act of kindness, every gesture of generosity? I am so hardwired to expect that whatever appreciation I show will be insufficient that I'd rather avoid the whole thing. No gifts for me, thanks. And when I'm on the giving end I try to fight what I believe is the calculus of the world—that we give in order to get—but I can't help it, I still want to feel appreciated.

7. Empathy versus Pity: Trying to tell the difference between empathy and pity has been onerous for me. My mother's unrelenting need for pity was so bare that I seem to have developed a phobic response to the whole idea of anything that smacks of that sort of energy. Yes, I am a psychologist and I spend my days offering empathy, that it's the keystone

of this work I have freely chosen. It is a bit of a puzzle. That pathway—the empathy *out* pathway—is etched deep for sure and, thank you mom, I have had a perfect career because of it. When it's *me* though, when I am struggling or in need, I recoil. The world is out there ready to judge me as pathetic and pitiable which I find close to unbearable.

8. Writing a Memoir: In theory I do believe that we all have a story to tell; that we are each entitled to the space we take up on this planet; that each of our voices should be heard. But the decision to commit my story to paper and send it out into the world has been fraught. Feeling entitled myself to have a story worth telling, that my life is worth the ink, feels perilously close to believing that I am extraordinary. A whole book about me! After all, when you write a book where "I" is the topic, isn't that *prima facie* proof that you, too, are a narcissist?

9. Healthy Narcissism: There's this old Hasidic tale I heard: When a child is born, the rabbi says you are to place one piece of paper in each pocket. One reads: *The world is made for you.* The other says: *You are but a speck of dust in the universe.* No

doubt this is a challenge on its face but it is probably the central challenge for children of narcissistic parents, being able to hold both of those seemingly contradictory truths at the same time. Without the esteem and confidence that comes with a healthy level of self-regard, how able are we to meet the rigors of any life? It's vital to feel gratitude for your gifts and to take pleasure in a job well done. True, healthy narcissism is necessary for a secure sense of self but for folks like me, any old kind of narcissism can freak us out. It rings that same old bell and that's downright terrifying. It's like a grease-lined slippery slope straight down to Crazy Town.

70

Hello Sister (2005 to present)

ON MARCH 8TH OUR MOTHER DIES AND ON March 9th it is as though some invisible barrier disintegrates just like that. My sister and me. Together. Alone. Without our mother. Weird.

It seems there always had to be one good daughter and one bad daughter. That's just Triangulating 101. And, no surprise, as long as our mother was alive my sister and I each held up one end of a polarizing stick. My end of the stick was the "mom is nuts" end and my sister's was the "mom needs our compassion" end. But now there seems to be no stick at all and we find ourselves together in a big old stew of compassion and hair-pulling exasperation. Still, the way my mother would complain to each of us about the other. How deep and insidious and primitive is the desire to be the chosen one.

Goodbye, mom.

We find a small patch of grass on Telegraph Hill just under Coit Tower where our very shrewd mother had led her whipped husband by the nose into what would turn out to be a spectacular real estate investment. There it is, just down the hill, the Victorian they turned into a triplex, how she walked up and down these hills, schlepping her string bag of groceries and the bargains she found in North Beach and Chinatown.

We sit close to each other looking east across the bay, me in my jeans and, I am sure, a black top of some kind; my sister looking more pulled together, wearing those beautiful pearl drop earrings she always wears. We don't usually get pegged as sisters. Besides the differences in our basic styles, she's fair and blue-eyed, a couple of inches shorter than I. My hair, almost black, is a mass of curls. I look more like our father; she, more like our mother. Could that explain everything? But sitting there so close to her is a comfort I didn't even know I needed. We lean in shoulder to shoulder. How we start talking is with a kind of "at least" tone. "She was always the Brownie troop leader," my sister says, "she taught us all to make hospital corners." I say, "And all those crazy doll clothes." It's clear enough to see all the way to Marin County and for a while we sit and watch the boats moving under the bridge. "She was a really good cook," my sister says. It's as though the blue sky and the red bridge and the green hills and the still water are there to remind us. Good things. How she taught us to love entertaining; how we knew music and art and theater and books; how every Thanksgiving she'd invite foreign dignitaries who worked at the U.N. to join us; how people were so charmed by her. Remind us, yes, we were grateful.

Then my sister says, "That was so *her*. With the doctor." "Amazing," I think we say at the exact same time. On that last day, my mother lay eyes closed, mute, non-responsive—non-responsive, that is, until the thirty-year-old resident came in the room at which point she scooched herself up, smiled big, and—please-God-no—showed a little leg, saying something about isn't he adorable, why are all the doctors so young and cute, do you have to leave so soon? Everyone in the hospital loved my mother, including the cute resident so he says something flirty back, does his thing and leaves, and—boom—she's out again. Just like that. Those were the last words we heard from her, the last human interaction she had on this good earth, even as we sat in her room for the rest of the day. So perfectly her.

Goodbye, mom.

"It reminds me of the lunch with her when she first moved into that place," I say. "Remember? You and I sitting there in the dining room and she goes on and on about how the luckiest people there were the ones who had sons." We're struck speechless there at the top of Telegraph Hill, just like we were in that dining room. Speechless.

And then we talk about how her death gives us the space to release our love and compassion and how very tragic that is for us all, how she seemed bound and determined to make it impossible for us to access those feelings in her presence and why did she have to do that to us. Why, why, why.

We head down the hill toward the triplex and do a cursory scout to make sure that whoever lives there now can't see us hovering around their property. My sister opens her purse and pulls out a Ziploc bag. We each reach in and leave a handful of our mother's ashes around the foundation of the house.

Goodbye, mom.

Next stop: Yank Sing. We all love Chinese food and we all love Yank Sing the best. My mother took a particularly proprietary attitude toward Yank Sing, like she had discovered it or invented it or was the only one on earth who knew about it. We went there every time I came to visit and it's where my kids went to fetch an enormous order of take-out to bring to the hospital, practically everything on the menu, in an effort to please the dying woman. For my sister and me it was something to get used to, ordering without her there. *Get whatever you want, everything's fantastic. Oh you want that? Did you see the price? Besides, you should get this instead, it's really much better. I've been here a thousand times so I should know. Here, just let me order.* So my sister and I choose with impunity like prisoners ordering up a last meal.

The first round of food arrives: Phoenix shrimp, stuffed lotus leaf, and pea shoot dumplings. It's hard to know what's more compelling: the ethereal morsels in front of us or why we're here in the first place. My sister brings a dumpling to her mouth, expert with chopsticks. "Do you remember that Christmas?" I say. "When I gave you the skirt?" My sister, her mouth full, looks puzzled, shakes her head no. She doesn't remember. Too young, I guess, probably around seven, to my twelve or thirteen. And really it's more my story anyway. Christmas morning and it was the three of us, my mother, my sister, and me in the house my father never lived in. I had learned to sew. For my mother I made a dark grapey-purple soft wool cape lined in pale gray silk and a matching pair of pants. For my sister, a red watch plaid long skirt with a black velvet waistband. How my mother reacted to her gift is strangely not an issue for me though I do have a vague memory of feeling hurt when she opened the box, held it up, maybe said something non-committal, and then put that purple suit right back in the box where it stayed, never to be seen or heard of again. I kind of get it. If my twelve-year-old kid made me a friggin' purple pantsuit, man would that be a pickle. I would, of course, ooh and ahh which my mother did *not* do. I would fling the cape over my shoulders and list all the places I would wear it but what a dilemma it would be, no? I get that. But what really lives in me from that day is this: my sister opens her present and she's so happy she actually shrieks and wants to put the skirt on right over her Cinderella pajamas and then says she wants to wear it to the Christmas party we are all going to later that day but my mother tells her no, she already has a nice dress picked out she can wear and don't bother trying it on, she should just put the skirt back in the box and it too was never seen or heard of again.

The rest of our order arrives: lobster dumplings, sea bass roll, and pork siu mai—stuff my mother would never have ordered, do you see the price on that! We each stick a chopstick into a dumpling and my sister shakes her head and says, "Mussolini." The Mussolini moment has got to be one of my top ten life moments. There we were, sitting on either side of our mother's hospital bed on that last afternoon. I lean across and whisper because who knows whether this is a real coma or a fake coma or even a fake dying. "You won't believe what I found," I said. "In her stuff." My sister leans toward me so we are face to face, that close. "In this folder, it said VALUABLE PHOTOS, Jesus Christ, it was Mussolini. Fucking Mussolini, naked, hung by his feet, upside down, dead. And another one, Mussolini fucking naked on a slab at the morgue. Fucking naked Mussolini, glossy eight by tens, what the fuck!" We both try hard to keep our laughter quiet and then my sister comes in even closer and says, "Do you think she had anything to do with it?"

There are two massive potted plants at the entrance to the restaurant. With supreme craftiness and duplicity, which I am sure we can attribute to our mother, we sidle up to the giant bamboo, looking ever so not-up-to-anything. My sister holds her open purse behind her back and we each extract another handful of ashes that go right into the pots. Both of us rub our hands on our jeans to wipe off the dry ash but some remains, soaked deep in our skin.

Goodbye, mom.
Hello, sister.

71

Last Words (2005)

MY LAST WORDS TO MY MOTHER, HOURS BEFORE she died—whether she heard me in her state I have no idea—leaning in, my face up to hers in a closeness that in our lives together would have been unbearable: "Mother, you have been infuriating to me my whole life. Utterly infuriating. But, I am very glad you were my mother."

Because you exposed me to art and theater and music and museums...

...so these things have been important, enriching, and central pursuits in my life.

Because you provided me with all the material comfort I could ever need...

…so I never needed to struggle financially and was able to have so many experiences without the worry of needing to find a way to pay for them.

Because you were unconventional…

…so orthodoxy has never been of much importance to me.

Because you needed the world to believe that your daughters were the smartest, prettiest, most-talented…

…so that false belief shored up my self-esteem until I was capable of developing a more realistic sense of myself.

Because I was never concerned about pleasing you…

…so I made my own decisions without worry about getting your input or approval.

Because I had all the freedom I wanted…

…so I was exposed early to all manner of adult experiences.

Because you surrounded yourself and us with interesting people…

…so I have a broad, catholic understanding and acceptance of humanity.

Because you were a boy-crazy woman…

…so I have had a checkered, mixed-bag, balls-to-the-wall history with men.

Because you valued reading and writing…

…so I took for granted that people read and then I ultimately found my way to writing.

Because you were relaxed about entertaining…

…so I look forward to having people in my own home and never stress about it.

Because every gift you gave, every favor you conferred, every gesture you made came with strings attached…

…so I meticulously scrutinize my motives with any offering and only give when I am 1000% sure I can give freely.

Because you were wily and shrewd and tough and dogged…

…so I have always believed that women are strong and able.

Because your moral compass—if you ever even had one—was out of commission…

…so I know when I can game the system, don't put much stock in rules, and have kept a watchful eye on any impulse to lie or cheat or beguile.

Because you paid for the college I chose to go to, never once asked me what I wanted to study, and never once expressed interest or concern about what I planned to do with my life…

…so I fucked around in college, never once concerned that a BA in Art History (which I was only marginally interested in anyway) was worth nothing and thinking about what I really wanted to do with my life didn't happen until I was close to thirty at which point I had a little more life under my belt so I was in a better position to decide than if I'd had to figure that out when I was a nearly unconscious, decidedly late bloomer.

Because you started multiple businesses and engaged in so many creative money-making projects…

…so I have a strong you're-not-the-boss-of-me personality and have had a lifetime of being my own boss.

Because you were chronically depressed, often alluded to suicide, and felt free to express every grim self-assessment you had…

…so I have never been surprised or put off when I encounter anyone's dark side, including my own.

Because you kept your past so hidden…

…so I decided to be as open and transparent as possible.

Because you were creative…

…so I have presumed that creative people were the best people and, in spite of believing that I was short-changed in that area, have surrounded myself with creative people throughout my life.

Because you had a very tenuous relationship with the truth…

…so I made honesty one of my foremost values.

Because you were mentally unstable and the man you married was at least as mentally unstable as you, and between the two of you we were left with a superfluity of unanswered questions…

…so the focus of my life has been a quest to understand the nuttiness, try to solve the puzzles, and look deep for answers, all of which led me instinctively, almost blindly, to what has turned out to be the most perfect career for me.

72

Passover

I'M SETTING THE TABLE FOR TEN, SQUEEZING TWO folding chairs at the corners, using the small placemats so everything will fit. It will be my little family and our faithful friends, the steadfast who join us for our handful of birthday celebrations every year, who come to the Oscar party and the movie nights. And every year a straggler or two. I don't have an official candlestick for the ceremony, I keep thinking I should get one, next year I'll get one for sure. This is our Seder. It's the fourth or fifth I've had which makes it the fourth or fifth I've been to.

On top of each plate is an Haggadah, our script for the evening. Ours is eight pages long, beginning and ending with a poem or a saying, maybe Rumi or Rilke or Mary Oliver or the Buddha, it changes every year. I've heard all the jokes about families starving their way through hour upon hour of detail upon detail, how we suffered and they tried to kill us and we survived, reading and chanting with nothing to eat except parsley dipped in salt water. Even the short Haggadahs out there would take a good two hours to get through before the Red Sea is parted and you are allowed to eat. No way would my group sit still for that.

So I wrote my own Haggadah. I combed through some of the longer, more earnest, more traditional. I scanned the feminist, the New Age, the Buddhist, and the recovery Haggadahs. They are long—fifty or sixty pages—and there's a lot of God in there, well, really Yah, or Adonai or HaShem or God written like this: G-d—since it seems that Judaism believes that writing, um, his name could get you in a boatload of trouble. This I learned getting ready for my first Seder.

For ours, the Passover story is about as abbreviated as I could make it. God is in there a couple of times, but only a couple, otherwise none of us would feel like it was ours. In the plagues section I've replaced the frogs and lice and boils and locusts with injustice, intolerance, prejudice, and violence. There is a place for us to reflect on how we keep our own selves enslaved, something I highly doubt would have been included in the texts used by my ancestors. And I actually don't know if it is kosher to laugh at a Seder, what with the persecution and exile and slavery and all those nasty plagues, but we always find the jokes.

My personal history of Seder dinner does not include memories of relatives arriving with covered dishes. I have not inherited a Seder plate stored away for that once-a-year dinner. I don't know all the details of the Passover story and I need my real Jewish friend to say the blessing. There is no echo from my childhood here but I see my need in this ritual and in what I have chosen to include. I think of all the ways I am enslaved—by past hurts and disappointments, by the pain of what I will never have, by the losses I still grieve. I vow to liberate myself and I hope all of us at the table are doing the same thing. At our Seder we close our eyes for a moment to remember the gone people in our lives. I think of my husband, my last and true love, and feel the clench of knowing that it has not been my karma, my fate, my good fortune to know a long and good marriage, and that now my heart may have been broken just one too many times. I think of my parents, recast in the forgiving relief of time and distance and feel my arms around them and my head resting on their shoulders, one then the other. And, if I hold a second longer, I see the faint line of the strangers that came before—my grandparents and their parents and the parents before them, all forming such a strong and straight line—and for a moment I feel a trace of ballast.

It's getting dark and everyone will be arriving soon. My place smells of the brisket that's been cooking all afternoon. Tonight I will be happy. Tonight I will be disappointed. Tonight we will laugh. We will be moved. We will be annoyed by each other but not say a word. I will feel the semblance of connection and I will feel its absence and not know if the absence is mine alone or something we each feel in our solitary souls as we sit together around this table. This is who I am. I am sometimes connected, sometimes not. Not the smartest, prettiest, most-talented. Not faultless or to blame. Tonight I am in line with this invisible chain of people who are at once strangers yet hugely a part of me; people I have never met and only recently even knew about, but who hold my hand and keep me tethered to this earth.

In some very important sense this is not my holiday. But I will light the tea lights scattered across the table and I will open the door for my welcomed guests.

Acknowledgments

To University of Hell Press, Greg Gerding and Eve Connell, dream editor-extraordinaire and all-round badass: thank you for welcoming me into the fold.

To my first teachers—Carolyn Altman and especially Tom Spanbauer, Dangerous Writing guru and hands down best teacher I've ever had in anything, period, end of story: thank you for opening this world to me.

To the most awesome Henry Writing Group—Robert Hill, David Ciminello, Gigi Little, Steve Arndt, Laura Stanfill, Sara Guest, Margaret Malone, Dian Greenwood, and Kathleen Lane (banana!): I'm deeply grateful for this space we have created to laugh and learn and hold. I love you guys!

To Tom Spanbauer, Rene Denfeld, Deborah Reed, Robert Hill, Margaret Malone, and Dianah Hughley: blessings for your blurby generosity. And Gigi Little: your artistic chops are beyond!

To Donna: So much gratitude! Without you, well, I just don't know!

To my sister: Girl, when you write your memoir (which I will read with my hands over my eyes!) I hope I have your equanimity and ability to accept what I am sure is a big bundle of uncomfortable. Hello, sister. I love you.

To Ashley and Erica: I've learned more about myself, about life, and about love from you both than I could have learned in any other way. I wish I knew then what I know now. I love you this much!

Liz Scott lives in Portland, Oregon where she is a
clinical psychologist in private practice by day and a
writer of both fiction and non-fiction.

THIS BOOK IS ONE OF THE
MANY AVAILABLE FROM
UNIVERSITY OF HELL PRESS.
DO YOU HAVE THEM ALL?

by **Leah Noble Davidson**
Poetic Scientifica
DOOR

by **Rory Douglas**
The Most Fun You'll Have at a Cage Fight

by **Brian S. Ellis**
American Dust Revisited
Often Go Awry

by **Greg Gerding**
The Burning Album of Lame
Venue Voyeurisms: Bars of San Diego
Loser Makes Good: Selected Poems 1994
Piss Artist: Selected Poems 1995-1999
The Idiot Parade: Selected Poems 2000-2005

by **Lauren Gilmore**
Outdancing the Universe

by **Rob Gray**
The Immaculate Collection/The Rhododendron and Camellia Year Book (1966)

by **Joseph Edwin Haeger**
Learn to Swim

by **Lindsey Kugler**
HERE.

by **Wryly T. McCutchen**
My Ugly & Other Love Snarls

by **Michael McLaughlin**
Countless Cinemas

by **Johnny No Bueno**
We Were Warriors

by **Isobel O'Hare**
all this can be yours

by **A.M. O'Malley**
Expecting Something Else

by **Stephen M. Park**
High & Dry
The Grass Is Greener

by **Christine Rice**
Swarm Theory

by **Michael N. Thompson**
A Murder of Crows

by **Sarah Xerta**
Nothing to Do with Me

edited by **Cam Awkward-Rich & Sam Sax**
*The Dead Animal Handbook: An Anthology of
Contemporary Poetry*

CPSIA information can be obtained
at www.ICGtesting.com
Printed in the USA
FSHW020140121019
62873FS